effective
Literacy
Practice
in Years 1 to 4

Effective Literacy Practice
in Years 1 to 4

Ministry of Education

Learning Media
Wellington

Published 2003 for the Ministry of Education by
Learning Media Limited, Box 3293, Wellington, New Zealand.
www.learningmedia.co.nz

Dewey number 372.6
ISBN 0 478 12940 8
Item number 12940

Distributed in the United States by:

Richard C. Owen Publishers, Inc.
PO Box 585
Katonah, NY 10536
1-800-336-5588/www.Rcowen.com

Contents

Ensuring that all students achieve good strengths in literacy is critical to their subsequent success in education and throughout their lives. Increasing the effectiveness of teaching practice in this critical area is therefore a priority. This publication is an important contribution to increasing the range of quality resources and information available to teachers. It has been designed as the key reference for professional development programmes as well as providing a platform for further materials to support literacy teaching and learning in classrooms. It builds from the work of the 1998 Government-appointed Literacy Taskforce. This Taskforce provided advice that was a key input into the development of the Literacy and Numeracy Strategy.

The Literacy Taskforce focused on ways to ensure that all children receive the best possible teaching in the first four years at school. Included in its report were recommendations that:

- A statement of best practice be drawn up and promulgated to schools. This statement should also guide the Ministry of Education's development and distribution of curriculum materials for both children and teachers and guide schools' purchases of materials.
- *Reading in Junior Classes* be revised.

Effective Literacy Practice in Years 1 to 4 has been developed in response to those recommendations and is integral to the ongoing implementation of the Government's Literacy Strategy.

During the development of this handbook, surveys of research have highlighted the extent to which effective teaching practice influences learning outcomes. It is now very clear that effective teaching is the single largest system influence on the achievement of all students. In order to be as effective as possible, teachers need access to quality resources and information.

Research also highlights a number of important dimensions that contribute to effective teaching practice. The statement of effective literacy practice that this book articulates is informed by evidence. It focuses on those dimensions of effective practice that are identified in both New Zealand and international studies.

I would like to thank all those people who have been involved in producing this handbook. The process of development and consultation has involved many teachers, academics, researchers, and policy makers. The result is a handbook that links literacy teaching practice and learning processes, providing advice that we can be confident will lead to improved outcomes for students.

Howard Fancy
Secretary for Education

Chapter 1:
A Focus on Effective Practice

Why focus on effective practice?

The focus of this book is on effective literacy teaching practice – that is, on what the classroom teacher does that leads to improved outcomes for students. The influence of the teacher on students' learning has long been recognised. Teachers matter, and what they do matters.

Competing claims about how best to teach reading and writing sharpen our awareness of what teachers do and help to focus attention on classroom practice. However, clear evidence of the most effective features of instructional practice has been documented. We can be confident not only about the degree of the teacher's influence but also about what it is that teachers do that makes a difference to student outcomes.

Teaching practice can be described as truly effective only when it has a positive impact on student achievement. This book aims to help teachers serve the needs of all learners in New Zealand's classrooms by showing teachers the evidence that links literacy teaching practice, learning processes, and student outcomes.

The evidence about effective practice in literacy

The evidence has integrity; it is credible and consistent. It is possible to be precise about what makes a difference to students' literacy learning. Certain features of teaching practice have been clearly linked to improved outcomes for students and to reduced disparities in the achievement of diverse groups of students. The evidence that makes these links arises from research studies, in New Zealand and internationally, that meet criteria for validity and reliability.

There are many studies of exemplary practice from which researchers, theorists, and practitioners have drawn conclusions about what constitutes best literacy teaching practice. Some of the key documents are identified at the end of this chapter. Wide agreement has been reached across a broad range of experts and groups with varying perspectives on literacy teaching and learning. The dimensions of effective practice, on which the chapter structure of this book is based, have been informed by this evidence.

Teaching practice can make a major difference to student outcomes. A synthesis of research states:

> *Our best evidence ... is that what happens in classrooms through quality teaching and through the quality of the learning environment generated by the teacher and the students, is the key variable in explaining up to 59%, or even more, of the variance in student scores.*

> Ministry of Education, 2003a, page 8

This shift in focus towards effective teaching practice builds on and gives a new emphasis to New Zealand's long-held tradition of child-centred learning.

Equity and diversity

Although children take many pathways in their literacy learning, teachers can apply the features of quality teaching practice effectively for all their students. This is a key message of *Effective Literacy Practice in Years 1 to 4*. The ways in which teachers use instructional strategies and activities or put programmes together will vary. However, all teachers can bring a sharper focus to their practice, provide goal-directed literacy instruction, and become better informed about ways of helping students from a wide range of backgrounds to make progress in their learning.

There is an ongoing search, internationally, for ways of delivering education that will result in more equitable outcomes for all students in schools. The work of New Zealand educators and researchers has made a significant contribution to this activity. The results of both international and local studies focus attention on educators' responsibility towards all students and on the possibilities for improving all students' learning.

Regular classroom teachers can develop their expertise – they can deliver effective literacy instruction. Their ideas and expectations about their effectiveness and children's capacity to achieve are important. A major hurdle for them is to be prepared to take responsibility for the outcomes of their teaching, not to believe that factors in the home and the child are the cause for lack of progress.

Keith, 2002, page 12 (summarising Phillips, McNaughton, and MacDonald, 2000)

This focus is of particular significance for New Zealand, given the increasing diversity of students in New Zealand classrooms and associated disparities in literacy achievement. Research has shown that some groups of students have not been well served by the conventional literacy practices in our schools (even though these practices have placed New Zealand in the top bracket of literacy achievement in international surveys).[1] The patterns have been well documented: Māori children, Pasifika children, children whose home language is not English, and children in low-decile schools achieve, on average, at a lower level than other children. Initial disparities tend to increase during subsequent years at school. This book discusses the features of effective practice that help to reduce these disparities.

We have acquired a great deal of knowledge about what is needed to reduce disparities in achievement. One landmark project in New Zealand, an intervention based on professional development for teachers, resulted in improved achievement by Māori and Pasifika children in a group of low-decile schools in South Auckland. The authors of the study (Phillips, McNaughton, and MacDonald, 2000) conclude that the historical pattern of low progress is neither inevitable nor immutable.

The features of effective practice described in this book can be applied to the range of student needs, including the needs of boys and girls, the talented or gifted, students from diverse backgrounds, students learning English as a new language, and students experiencing difficulties in their literacy learning.

Continuity of literacy development

This book discusses literacy teaching and learning in English, with a focus on the first four years of instruction. It is important to view these years of the child's literacy development in the context both of the years before formal instruction and of subsequent years of schooling. A number of studies have highlighted:

- the importance of the child's experiences and engagement in literacy activities prior to starting school and when they start school;
- the significance of the transition to school in terms of a child's learning;
- the importance of meeting the needs of those whose home literacy practices differ from those of the school;
- the fact that children take different pathways towards becoming literate.

Much of the information in this book is relevant beyond the first four years, and certainly the dimensions of effective practice apply across all year groups.

---

[1] Studies that provide this evidence are listed at the end of this chapter.

As students move through the school, teachers face the challenge of both maintaining their students' motivation and progress and reducing the disparities between the achievements of different groups. Teachers of students beyond year 4 will find helpful guidance in this book as they work to meet these challenges.

A range of influences on achievement

Many factors impact on individual students' achievements, on the patterns of progress in particular classes, and on patterns across the school. Some of these factors are of a personal nature, relating to students' feelings of being successful or capable or to their personal interests. There are also many social, economic, and cultural forces that together contribute to other factors (such as transience) that affect students' learning and influence the nature and scope of their opportunities and experiences both in and out of school.

The challenge for teachers is to accept responsibility in the face of such realities and commit themselves to realising the best outcomes for all their students. Many inspiring stories provide evidence of some teachers' success in circumstances that have long been considered – and often subconsciously accepted – as barriers to achievement. Teachers who are well informed and well equipped can be confident about what they can do to meet the challenges and address the issues.

Quality interactions

This book is not just about excellence in teaching practice or expertise in the cognitive processes involved in becoming a reader and writer, vital as these are. Studies have demonstrated the interdependence of personal, social, and academic aspects of the student's well-being.[2] Connecting with students makes for quality classroom interactions and relationships.

The teacher's ability to build quality relationships with students and among students is crucial. This ability is based on the teacher's knowledge and awareness of how learners acquire literacy.

Effective teachers create environments that facilitate learning because they have a culture of shared understandings and shared values, such as caring and welcoming diversity. When the teacher's own passion shines through the literacy activities of the classroom, it affects the quality of the students' learning. What counts most is what teachers do, moment by moment, in their interactions with their students.

---

[2] For a summary of the evidence in these studies, see Ministry of Education (2003a), pages 19–27.

The dimensions of effective literacy practice

Chapters 2 to 7 of this book discuss the dimensions of effective practice. Each chapter defines one dimension and discusses how it relates to teachers' practice and students' achievement. The final chapter discusses important considerations for shaping classroom literacy programmes and building learning communities. It also includes case studies at various levels.

The Dimensions of Effective Practice

Knowledge of literacy learning

Knowledge of literacy learning encompasses knowledge about literacy as well as knowledge about literacy acquisition. Literacy is the ability to understand, respond to, and use those forms of written language that are required by society and valued by individuals and communities.

Teachers need an extensive and continually developing knowledge of:

- the theoretical and research base about teaching, learning, and the process of becoming literate;
- the repertoire of reading and writing strategies, and the knowledge and awareness, that learners need to develop as they acquire literacy;
- instructional strategies and their effective use.

Knowledge of the learner

Knowledge of the learner encompasses knowing about the pathway of progress for each child and about the patterns of progress for literacy learners in general at different points in their development.

Teachers need an extensive and continually developing knowledge of:

- each child's individual profile of learning and the implications of this for instruction;
- patterns of progress for learners as they acquire literacy;
- each child's language and literacy practices outside of school as well as in school.

This knowledge:

- is gathered in a planned way from many sources, formal and informal;
- is analysed and used to inform practice;
- involves sensitivities relating to individual learners, such as cultural considerations or rates of progress.

The effective gathering, analysing, and using of knowledge about the learner is informed by the teacher's knowledge of literacy learning as well as by the teacher's expectations.

Instructional strategies

Instructional strategies are the tools of effective practice. They are the deliberate acts of teaching that focus learning in order to meet a particular purpose.

Teachers use instructional strategies when:

- activating prior knowledge (for example, by questioning to link a child's relevant experience with the text to be read or written);
- setting a purpose (for example, to write clearly about personal experiences);

- explicitly and systematically teaching word analysis (for example, by prompting the learner to decode and encode unfamiliar words through letter and sound analysis);

- teaching ways of comprehending text (for example, by developing the learner's awareness of inference to enable them to make meaning in reading and writing);

- modelling the processes of being an effective reader and writer (for example, by thinking aloud about how word meanings can be constructed in reading or by selecting appropriate words to convey meaning in writing);

- providing feedback (for example, by specifically commenting on the quality and appropriateness of features of what a learner has read or written, to provide direction for new learning).

The teacher's use of instructional strategies is informed by their knowledge of the learner and of literacy learning. Effective teachers plan the use of instructional strategies, and they also make strategic, "on the run" decisions in the course of their teaching.

Effective teachers use the instructional strategies within a range of contexts and approaches to teaching reading and writing:

- reading to children;
- guided reading and writing;
- shared reading and writing;
- independent reading and writing;
- other contexts.

These have been developed as ways of using instructional strategies to guide learners and provide them with opportunities for learning. Effective teachers use a mix of these contexts and approaches to achieve a balanced programme for their students.

Engaging learners with texts

Engaging learners with texts means placing the use and creation of texts at the heart of literacy learning. Texts exist and can be created in written, oral, and visual forms.

Effective practice in engaging literacy learners with texts involves:

- using and creating a variety of appropriate texts in reading and writing;
- knowing the language features of texts;
- both teachers and learners understanding the purposes of using and creating texts;
- enabling learners to integrate their knowledge, awareness, and repertoire of strategies in using and creating texts;
- making links between reading and writing;
- including contemporary and evolving ways of using and creating texts.

Effective practice involves using and creating rich texts. These relate to children's interests, draw on and affirm their social and cultural identities, use authentic language, and motivate and challenge them as learners.

Expectations

Expectations are the ideas that teachers, children, parents, and communities have about children as learners – about their knowledge and expertise, their progress, and their achievement.

Teachers' expectations are shaped by:
- their beliefs and values;
- their professional and theoretical knowledge.

Teachers' expectations for learners should be high but appropriate and should also be:
- clearly expressed;
- shared with all partners in the child's learning and informed by feedback from all partners;
- reflected upon and reviewed.

Teachers' expectations shape all aspects of their practice. They impact on learners' patterns of progress as well as on their achievement.

Partnerships

Partnerships are collaborative relationships that contribute to and support children's learning. Each learner lives in a network of significant people, including their teachers, family, peers, and specialist teachers. Effective teachers recognise the need for, and actively promote, partnerships within these networks.

Effective partners complement one another and value one another's contributions. Each partner has a particular role in the relationship.

Partnerships depend on:
- shared expectations;
- shared knowledge about the learner;
- shared knowledge about literacy learning;
- all partners knowing and valuing the learner's background of experience, including home literacy practices.

Effective partnerships are active, planned, and dynamic.

Further reading

For full reference details of the resources listed here, refer to pages 189–194.

A synthesis of research about effective practice, highly relevant to literacy teaching and learning, is:

Ministry of Education (2003a). *Quality Teaching for Diverse Students in Schooling: Best Evidence Synthesis.*

Studies and statements about exemplary literacy teaching practice and influences on learning include:

Braunger, J. and Lewis, J. (1998). *Building a Knowledge Base in Reading.*

Cambourne, B. (2000). "Conditions for Literacy Learning: Observing Literacy Learning in Elementary Classrooms: Nine Years of Classroom Anthropology".

Hattie, John (1999). "Influences on Student Learning".

Medwell, J., Wray, D., Poulson, L., and Fox, R. (1998). *Effective Teachers of Literacy: Final Report to the Teacher Training Agency.*

Ministry of Education (1999a). *Literacy Experts Group Report to the Secretary for Education.*

Pressley, M., Allington, R. L., Wharton-McDonald, R., Block, C. C., and Morrow, L. M. (2001). *Learning to Read: Lessons from Exemplary First-grade Classrooms.*

Wilkinson, I. A. G. and Townsend, M. (2000). "From Rata to Rimu: Grouping for Instruction in Best Practice New Zealand Classrooms".

Reviews, research studies, and commentaries about literacy teaching and learning include:

Farstrup, A. E. and Samuels, S. J., eds (2002). *What Research Has to Say about Reading Instruction.*

National Institute of Child Health and Human Development (2000). *Report of the National Reading Panel: Teaching Children to Read: An Evidence-Based Assessment of the Scientific Research Literature on Reading and Its Implications for Reading Instruction.*

Rivalland, J. (2000). "Finding a Balance for the Year 2000 and Beyond".

Snow, C. (chair) and RAND Reading Study Group (2001). *Reading for Understanding: Toward an R & D Program in Reading Comprehension.*

Snow, C. E., Burns, S. M., and Griffin, P., eds (1998). *Preventing Reading Difficulties in Young Children.*

Documentation about literacy achievement levels in New Zealand and internationally is contained in such works as:

Flockton, L. and Crooks, T. (1999). *Writing Assessment Results 1998.*

Flockton, L. and Crooks, T. (2001). *Reading and Speaking Assessment Results 2000.*

International Association for the Evaluation of Educational Achievement (2000). *Framework and Specifications for PIRLS Assessment 2001: PIRLS Progress in International Reading Literacy Study.*

Ministry of Education (2001a). "Programme for International Student Assessment".

Pitches, N., Thompson, L., and Watson, S. (2002). *How Well Do New Zealand Children Read?*

Chapter 2:
Knowledge of Literacy Learning

Introduction

Knowledge of literacy learning encompasses knowledge about literacy as well as knowledge about literacy acquisition. The definition of literacy in this book is:

Literacy is the ability to understand, respond to, and use those forms of written language that are required by society and valued by individuals and communities.

Language and literacy

Effective Literacy Practice in Years 1 to 4 focuses on teaching students to read and write using the written forms of the English language. However, it is well established, through studies and theories of language learning, that oral language underpins written language; the two are closely interrelated. It is vital for children to listen and speak in order to develop a grasp of language. Through talking about events as they happen and discussing their ideas, children construct knowledge and awareness and acquire the language they need in order to make sense of their experiences. From their earliest years on into their school years, children benefit from many and varied opportunities to develop and practise oral language in their homes, communities, and classrooms. Their language is enriched when they interact in many contexts where supportive adults, including family, give them plenty of feedback and encouragement. Such interactions provide children with essential experience to build on when engaging with texts and delighting in them. However, instruction in reading and writing should not "wait" until a child has a strong oral language base.

Visual language is inherent in reading and writing. In order to find and create meaning in written language, students need to understand such features of visual language as the use of symbols and images to convey meaning.[3] For example, when students use computers to communicate even at a basic level, they need to be able to interpret the combinations of text and images in desktop icons and menus.

Contemporary environments

Teachers need to consider literacy teaching and learning in the light of changing social and cultural environments. Increasing numbers of communication forms, along with increasing cultural and linguistic diversity, have given rise to the concept of multiliteracies. It's useful to think in terms of a dynamic, shifting set of literacy practices that shape young learners, and indeed all people, as social beings. We need a broader view of literacy now than ever before.

The challenge for teachers is to increase students' control over and awareness of the ways in which the many communication forms can be used. Teachers can encourage their students to be reflective and discriminating and, at the same time, to enjoy the process of literacy learning.

Literacy practices are the ways in which literate people understand, respond to, and use language forms. Some of these practices are required and valued inside school, some are required and valued outside school, and some are common to many settings, both in and out of school.

---

[3] Further information about visual language and its features can be found on pages 173–222 of *Exploring Language*.

Literacy development: the theoretical basis

Effective practice has a theoretical basis that can be expressed in terms of three related concepts: a developmental perspective, a socialisation model, and the fact that children take individual and multiple pathways of development. An understanding of these concepts enables teachers to be informed and confident about their literacy teaching practice.

A developmental perspective

The child who arrives at school is on a pathway of development and has learned a great deal already. It is the business of schools to foster the processes of development in all learners. In the context of literacy learning, this means enabling learners to progress towards fluency and independence in using written forms of language. They do so through acquiring knowledge and strategies for literacy learning and awareness of how to use them.

The socialisation model

The socialisation model of literacy learning is built on the idea that the child constructs meaning within social settings. Social and cultural practices in fact shape all learning, and children's literacy development is shaped by their interactions with those around them. A process of socialisation begins at birth and continues through the school years and into adult life. This model is based on the concept of co-construction.[4]

A child's ways of constructing and their family's patterns of guidance are mutually composed, hence the term co-construction.

McNaughton, 2002, page 23

From their earliest years, children construct understandings through engaging in activities at home, in community settings, and at school. Families and communities develop shared ways of participating in these activities, based on shared understandings. Some activities are arranged specifically to help children learn. Children's interactions with other people during these activities are the means through which literacy learning takes place. The literacy practices that young children see used and valued by those closest to them become part of their own cultural identity and expertise.

Schools, as well as families and communities, have well-established literacy practices, and children learn to construct meanings within their school's pattern of guidance. The ways in which a teacher uses the curriculum, instructional strategies and approaches, and rich texts with students not only determine what the students learn but also shape their individual developmental pathways and their general patterns of progress. Students take part in literacy activities in a social situation (the classroom), drawing upon the teacher and the other students to help them construct understandings about texts and the ideas in the texts. The process is interactive: the students bring their expertise to share with others in these activities, and at the same time they develop new expertise. All students should find classroom literacy activities both enjoyable and challenging.

---

[4] The concept of co-construction has been described by Stuart McNaughton, drawing upon his own work (McNaughton, 1995, 1999, 2002) and that of Valsiner (1988) and Rogoff (1990).

Individual and multiple pathways of development

Each child is on a unique pathway of development. Although there is wide agreement that children can be expected to achieve certain outcomes at particular points in their progress (see pages 70–74), there are always variations in children's expertise and in their routes and rates of progress. A teacher who sees learning as a process of co-construction will recognise that there are multiple ways in which different children construct meanings and learn to use written forms of language.

The work of Marie Clay has been at the forefront in establishing the understanding that it is necessary for the teacher to work with what the child already knows and can control – what they are good at. At any point in a child's development, there is a sense in which their learning is a totality, right and whole for the child at that time. The child can be "engaged as an expert" in any literacy activity.

Implications for teachers

In summary, three related concepts underlie understandings about how children acquire literacy:

- The pathway to literacy is developmental.
- Social and cultural practices shape children's literacy learning.
- Children take individual and multiple pathways to literacy.

These are essential concepts for teachers to grasp. They highlight the uniqueness of the needs of each student, which is especially important in view of the diverse nature of school populations (see also page 46). An understanding of these concepts is essential for teachers planning literacy programmes, choosing learning activities, and being strategic in their teaching.

There is therefore no place for programmes with prescriptive methods and materials or for predetermined, recipe-style literacy activities that claim to fit the needs of all learners. There is no evidence of a single sequence of literacy development. The evidence shows clearly that there are many pathways that lead children to the desired goal of learning to read and write.[5]

Close recording of what children say reveals that they have traveled differently along the path of language acquisition, and they are not all at the same place in their learning: some have gone further than others. Their individual differences probably arose from different kinds of learning opportunities in their real-world contexts, and the only place to start further language development is to work with what they already control.

Clay, 1998, page 88

---

[5] For such evidence, see, for example, Snow, Burns, and Griffin (1998) and Clay (1998, 2001).

Motivation and engagement

Only when students are motivated, are interested, and enjoy learning do they make the progress they are capable of in their literacy learning and go on to become lifelong learners. An effective teacher connects to each student's interests, experiences, and sense of identity, shares a love of reading and writing, and generates excitement and a sense of purpose – all this gives heart to a teacher's practice. The teacher's practice should also be informed by knowledge about the role of motivation in the students' learning. (For evidence about the importance of motivation and engagement, refer to the end of this chapter.)

Motivation

Teachers have to create the conditions for motivation; it's not just a matter of immersing students in learning activities. When students are motivated and have developed the positive attitudes that will lead them to become independent readers and writers, they gain long-term benefits. Studies have shown that students' recreational reading and writing is a good indicator of their achievement.

Teachers' expectations for students' behaviour and academic performance influence the students' motivation and therefore their actual achievement (see chapter 6).

Students are more motivated when their learning activity is directed towards a goal that they know, when they receive informative and affirming feedback, and when they can see the links between what they did and successful outcomes.

Motivation is affected by self-concept and a sense of self-efficacy. A belief in themselves and their ability to succeed in classroom tasks has an energising effect on both teachers and students. This is why motivation is often a major issue for teachers working with students who have experienced difficulties in reading or writing.

Ultimately, our goal with students of diverse backgrounds, and with all students, is to promote ownership of literacy … Ownership has to do with valuing literacy, having a positive attitude toward literacy, and having the habit of using literacy.

Au, 2002, page 398

Students' motivation and engagement increase when they have ownership of their literacy learning and are familiar with the language and the tasks expected of them. This is especially so for those students whose backgrounds differ from that of the dominant school culture. When these learners' cultural values and knowledge are incorporated into their learning activities, they are more motivated to learn.

Engagement

Engagement means participating actively rather than being passive in the learning process. Learners engage more readily when they expect to succeed and when they see worthwhile challenge in their learning tasks.

In literacy learning, *intellectual engagement* relates to thinking – the cognitive processing of written forms of language. When learners engage intellectually, they bring mental rigour and focus to their learning task. As they read and write, they need to think consciously about how to use the knowledge and strategies they are acquiring.

Emotional engagement relates closely to motivation and interest and is important for both teachers and students. Literacy learners who are emotionally engaged will have a positive, sometimes even passionate, attitude towards reading and writing and will take ownership of their learning. Learners' emotional engagement is affected by other people's expectations and by their own self-concepts. When teachers and students are emotionally engaged in the learning, this enhances the quality of the relationships built between teachers and students and among students.

A further concept to consider is *cultural engagement*. Every learner views literacy tasks through a cultural "lens" because most of the prior knowledge, experiences, and values that a learner brings to literacy activities arise from their cultural background. Culturally based values and knowledge affect each learner's engagement and interest in the learning activity. Ensuring cultural engagement is particularly important in classrooms where the students come from diverse backgrounds, especially where their cultural backgrounds differ from the teacher's.

Literacy acquisition

The process of becoming literate is intensely complex. The literacy learner has to develop a knowledge base, a repertoire of strategies, and awareness of how to put their knowledge and strategies together. Students acquire literacy through planned activities that give them rich experiences with texts and related language activities. A knowledge of how learners acquire literacy underpins the teaching practice of effective teachers and gives them well-founded confidence.

A framework

In the framework for describing literacy acquisition that is outlined in this book, reading and writing are seen as having three aspects: learning the code, making meaning, and thinking critically.

Learning the code

This means developing the ability to decode and encode written forms of language. The focus is on the conventions of written language and the skills required to read and write letters, words, and text. "Cracking the code" is an exciting intellectual challenge for learners.

Making meaning

This involves developing and using knowledge, strategies, and awareness in order to get and convey meaning when reading or writing. It also involves understanding the forms and purposes of different texts and becoming aware that texts are intended for an audience.

Thinking critically

Becoming literate involves reading and writing beyond a literal, factual level. It involves analysing meanings, responding critically to text when reading, and being critically aware when composing texts. It also involves responding to texts at a personal level, reflecting on them, and finding reward in being a reader and a writer.

The three aspects

Although these three aspects are described separately above, they develop together during the process of becoming literate. Literacy learners need to become accurate and efficient in the actual business of reading and writing letters, words, and text. Learning the code is crucial. But it has no point unless it is the means to the essential end – reading and writing with meaning and purpose. At the same time, from the beginning of literacy instruction, students should be responding thoughtfully to the texts that they read and compose. For both students and their teachers, engaging actively in many text-based experiences that develop their literacy learning across these three aspects should provide daily enjoyment and challenge.[6]

---

[6] The three aspects of literacy acquisition described above are based on the model described by Luke and Freebody (1999).

A Framework for Literacy Acquisition

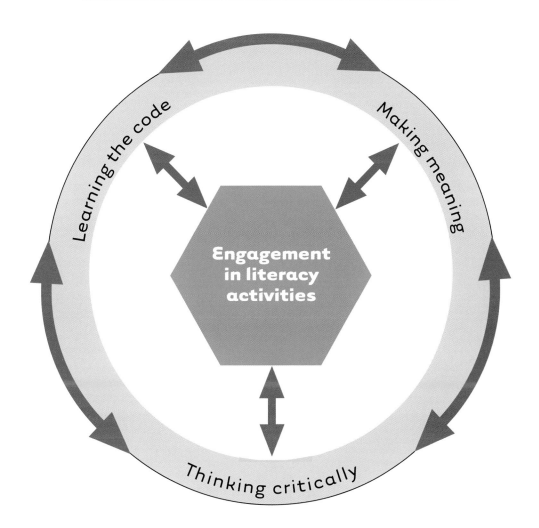

Learning the code

Making meaning

Engagement in literacy activities

Thinking critically

**With teacher support,
students develop knowledge and strategies
and also an awareness of how to use them
as readers and writers.**

The development of knowledge, strategies, and awareness

As they learn to decode and encode, to make meaning, and to think critically, learners develop knowledge, strategies, and awareness, which may be described as the core components of literacy development.

Learners need a continually increasing body of *knowledge* as they acquire literacy. This knowledge is of two kinds:

- background knowledge and experience – life experiences and general knowledge (see page 27);
- knowledge about reading and writing, how texts work, and how print works. The literacy-related knowledge that young learners need to develop is discussed on pages 27-37.

Learners need a repertoire of *strategies* for literacy. Readers and writers use various strategies in combination with their knowledge in order to decode and encode, make meaning, and think critically. For example, they use processing strategies (see page 38), comprehension strategies (see pages 40-41 and 131-134), and the strategies that are part of the writing process (see page 138-141).

Awareness is ... being able to attend to something, act upon it, or work with it.
Clay, 1998, page 42

Learners need to develop *awareness* of what they know and can do and how to deliberately apply and control their knowledge and strategies. This concept of awareness is inherent in the theory of literacy learning outlined on pages 20-21. For further discussion of the development of awareness, see pages 43-45.

Closely related to the concept of awareness is that of metacognition. This term is often used to describe the processes of thinking and talking about one's own learning. Being able to articulate what they know and can do helps students to set themselves new goals and meet new challenges.

Students develop knowledge, strategies, and awareness for literacy learning in an integrated way, not sequentially. For example, in order to attend to word-level information (a reading strategy), they draw on their knowledge of how print works and their awareness of phonics and letter forms. At the same time, working out words in these ways adds to their knowledge of how words are formed and to their awareness of effective strategies for solving words.

The development of learners' knowledge, strategies, and awareness does not occur during literacy sessions only. Learning occurs, and should be planned for, across all areas of the curriculum.

Developing knowledge for literacy learning

The knowledge that students need to develop for literacy learning includes background knowledge and literacy-related knowledge.

Background knowledge

Successful readers and writers do much more than process information. They bring their experience and existing knowledge, accumulated both in and out of school, to their reading and writing in order to construct meaning and develop new understandings.

As already discussed, children's knowledge is built within social and cultural settings, and there are socially determined patterns of knowledge. However, each learner's body of knowledge is unique; there are multiple pathways by which learners become literate.

The knowledge and experience that learners bring to their reading or writing, including the vocabulary they have developed, give them a starting point for connecting with a text or clarifying the ideas they seek to convey. Introducing a topic for shared writing or a text for guided reading by inviting conversation about the pictures and content, for example, helps young learners to make connections with what they already know.

The diversity among students in our schools presents a challenge for teachers – to identify and build upon the knowledge that all their students bring to the classroom. Teachers should always be aware that what the learner brings to the learning task is as important as what the teacher teaches.

Literacy-related knowledge

From their earliest attempts at reading and writing, children develop their literacy-related knowledge. As they begin formal instruction at school, they need to know how texts work (see below). They need to learn that spoken language is made up of sounds and words, to learn the spoken and written forms of the letters of the alphabet, and to understand that these relate to the sounds of spoken language (see pages 32–37). They also need to know about the visual features of print (see page 34).

Knowledge of how texts work

When children have frequent experiences of reading and writing, they begin to realise that there is a relationship between what they hear and the written text they create or read. Through listening to and talking about stories or through creating them, children learn the importance of sounds, of particular words, and of the flow and rhythm of language and story structure. They learn that words and the ways people say them can evoke an emotional response. They learn that texts can delight and inform and that it is worthwhile to listen to, to read, to view, and to create them.

Children learn that:
- texts have meaning and purpose;
- texts have a particular structure, according to their purpose;

- print is a written form of spoken language;
- the conventions of print are consistent;
- written text is constant.

This knowledge enables children to develop certain expectations and to make predictions about the form and structure of the text that they are going to read or write. Their knowledge of the purposes and structures of texts increases as they progress, enabling them to develop an analytical and thoughtful perspective as readers and writers.

Using sources of information in texts

Learners need to know how to use the sources of information in texts, along with their prior knowledge and experience, to decode and encode written English, make meaning, and think critically.

The three interrelated sources of information in written language that readers and writers use are:

- meaning (semantics) – the meanings of words and of images, such as pictures and diagrams, in their context;
- structure (syntax) – the grammatical structures of phrases and sentences;
- visual and grapho-phonic information, that is, the features of the printed letters, words, and punctuation – the visual aspects of the print itself.

These sources of information need to be considered in relation to one another.

Meaning: semantic sources of information

Children build up knowledge of words and their meanings through their experiences of spoken language in everyday life. Words acquire meaning in relation to the child's experience. Before they start school, children have absorbed the meanings of many words. They have learned the names of the people, objects, and events in their lives, and they have also learned to interpret subtle differences in meaning, for example, between "Sit up", "Sit down", and "Sit still".

Most will have a sense of English idiom (if English is their first language) and will understand that "Hang on a minute" does not imply holding on to anything.

Children who experience rich conversations with adults, siblings, and peers and who hear lots of stories and rhymes meet a great number of words in different contexts and build up a store of words they can use fluently. Some children's exposure to language may be more limited, and their vocabulary development may be slower. A child usually comes to understand what particular words mean through experience, but teachers can help to expand children's awareness of how words work by discussing the precise meanings of words as they arise in classroom activities, by planning text-based experiences (see chapter 5), and by encouraging quality conversations (see pages 88–89). Such experiences enable children to build a growing range of words that they will recognise in their reading and use in their writing.

Using illustrations with text helps learners to build meaning. Children's first writing is often captions for pictures; this develops their concepts about how pictures and words work together. The illustrations in a book may carry crucial information to help a young reader understand unfamiliar content and settings, or they may provide a subtext that offers a different perspective. In many factual texts, the photographs, illustrations, and diagrams are essential features for readers seeking a full understanding of the information.

Structure: syntactic sources of information

Children learn and develop language patterns from infancy. Well before a baby can distinguish or articulate a word, its babble imitates the "tune" of the language it hears. Later, as children learn to talk, their grammatical structures are mostly correct. Sometimes when they apply rules to make their meaning clearer, the results don't fit the irregularity of the English language but still demonstrate learning progress. For example, saying "Daddy rided", rather than "Daddy rode", shows an understanding of the standard form of the past tense in English.

Knowing the structure or syntax of a language helps readers to predict a word or the order of words in a sentence. A child who is using syntactic information knows what type of word is missing in the sentence "The dog _____ over the wall." The language of most five-year-olds enables them to use syntax well in predicting and checking the accuracy of words they read in their first language. Similarly, when children begin to write, they try to record what they might say. They are governed by syntax because the words we hear, speak, read, and write are organised into grammatical sequences. Children's understandings of written language structure increase progressively through planned literacy activities.

Visual and grapho-phonic sources of information

The term *visual information* refers to visual aspects of print, such as letters, words, spaces between words, and punctuation marks.

The term *visual language* is used to describe signs, symbols, illustrations, gestures, and so on that are used to communicate meaning.

Visual sources of information for readers are the visual features of the print itself. Visual information in a text includes letters, letter clusters, words, sentences, and the conventions of print, such as direction, spaces between words, the shapes of letters and words, and punctuation marks. It does not include illustrations.

The term "grapho-phonic information" encapsulates the idea that the information used to decode a printed word or to write a word is partly visual or graphic (the learner recognises the printed shape) and partly aural or phonic (the learner recreates the sounds of letters and words). The learner draws on prior knowledge to remember which visual configuration goes with which sound. Refer to page 32 for information about phonics and to pages 35–37 for information about letter-sound relationships.

When they write, students must attend to the detail of each word. They add to their store of knowledge about how certain visual shapes relate to certain sounds as they look closely at the features of letters and notice combinations of letters that occur often.

Integrating the sources of information in reading and writing

Fluent readers and writers draw on their prior knowledge and use all available sources of information simultaneously and usually unconsciously. Beginning readers and writers need to be taught to draw on these sources and to use them efficiently.

Hayley was reading the sentence "At last the wolf woke up". She read fluently until the written word "woke", which was unfamiliar. She recognised that the sentence structure required a verb and that the word began with "w", so she tried "walked". The next word, "up", was familiar, and Hayley realised that "walked up" would not make sense in this context, so she self-corrected to "woke up".

Students learn to use and integrate the sources of information effortlessly in their reading and writing when they have:

- a wide range of enjoyable books to hear and read;
- varied writing experiences;
- planned, explicit instruction by the teacher;
- many opportunities to develop their oral and written language;
- many opportunities to practise reading and writing an increasing range of texts that become progressively more challenging.

Further discussion and examples of effective instruction that enables learners to use and integrate the sources of information, along with their prior knowledge, may be found in chapter 4, Instructional Strategies, and chapter 5, Engaging Learners with Texts.

Note: Students learning English as a new language find it more difficult, initially, to use semantic and syntactic information in English. They are still developing their knowledge of the language that is associated with given contexts in written English and of the patterns of the English language. It is important that they are encouraged to develop such knowledge through oral language activities and supported in learning how to use visual and grapho-phonic information to decode and encode words so that they can read, write, and experience success.

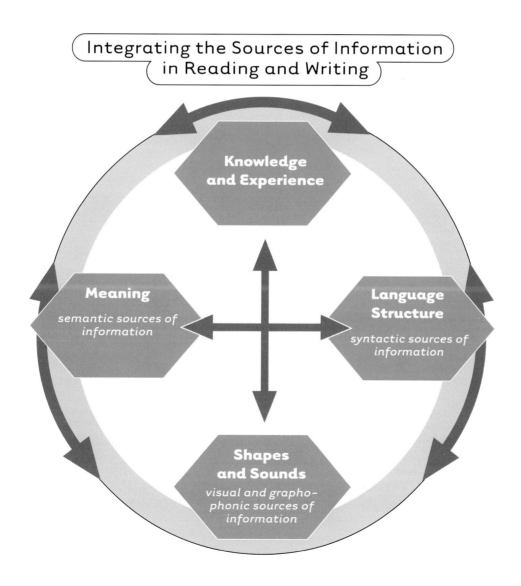

Integrating the Sources of Information in Reading and Writing

Knowledge and Experience

Meaning
semantic sources of information

Language Structure
syntactic sources of information

Shapes and Sounds
visual and grapho-phonic sources of information

Phonemic awareness and phonics

A *phoneme* is the smallest unit of sound in a word.

Phonemic awareness refers to the ability to hear, differentiate, and attend to the individual sounds within words.

Phonological awareness is a more inclusive term and refers to a general appreciation of the sounds of language or the general ability to attend to the sounds of language as distinct from its meaning.

In order to become readers and writers, children need to develop a knowledge of the names and sounds of the letters of the alphabet and of letter-sound relationships. Many children come to school already knowing the sounds commonly associated with some letters (especially the first letter of their name). As children learn to read and write, they develop much fuller understandings of how sounds relate to letters, letter clusters, and words. Teachers have a crucial role in teaching children how to draw on phonological knowledge, which is essential for decoding and encoding.

Children do not have to be able to name every letter of the alphabet before they begin formal instruction in reading and writing. They do, however, need to have developed phonemic awareness and to understand that there is a relationship between spoken sounds and the letters that represent them.

Phonemic awareness starts with distinguishing between words in a stream of speech. It then extends to being able to hear the phonemes, or individual sounds, in the words, that is, to recognise the difference between "thing" and "think"; "hint" and "hunt"; "bat" and "pat". Young children typically develop phonemic awareness through many experiences with oral language, especially with poems, jingles, rhymes, songs, and word games. Their phonemic awareness is also developed through writing.

Phonemic awareness is fundamental to early success in reading and writing. It enables children to develop the understanding of letter-sound relationships that is essential to decoding and encoding. Children have to be able to distinguish sounds before they can match them with the letters that represent them.

If children appear to have difficulty hearing and identifying sounds, they may have impaired hearing, and so a hearing check should be arranged.[7]

Phonics: the relationship between spoken sounds and the letters that represent them; the correspondence between sound and symbol in an alphabetic writing system.

An understanding of phonics also underpins children's literacy learning. Children need to learn, through deliberate, focused instruction, which letters represent which sounds. They learn a great deal about letter-sound relationships through writing. Beginning writers constantly engage with the problem of which letters represent the sounds in the words they want to use. In doing so, they lay a sound basis of knowledge about relationships between letters and sounds. Effective teaching helps students to transfer this knowledge to their reading and also to transfer back to their writing the understandings they gain during reading and oral language activities. (See the section on relating sounds to print, on pages 35–36.)

Through reading and writing activities, teachers help students to apply their growing understanding of phonics. As students gain more confidence and skill, they develop their knowledge and understanding further. They investigate more complex letter-sound relationships, for example, by discovering that one sound in English can be represented by different spellings: "**ch**aracter", "**k**itten", and "**c**astle"; "**ph**one", "cou**gh**", and "**f**air"; "**who**", "thr**ew**", and "thr**ough**". (See also the sections on grapho-phonic information, on page 30, and spelling, on pages 144–148.)

---

[7] Note that most children who are profoundly deaf cannot develop phonemic awareness in the way that hearing children do and will learn written English as a second language. Their first language is generally a signed language and, like all children, they achieve best when they establish learning in their first language before learning through the medium of a second language.

Refer also to the Ministry of Education's *Ready to Read Teacher Support Material: Sound Sense: Phonics and Phonological Awareness*.

Learning about print

All literacy learners need to: develop concepts about print, learn to read and write letters and words, learn about visual language in texts (including electronic texts), develop a sight vocabulary, learn to relate sounds to print and to relate parts of words to sounds, and apply their knowledge of letter-sound relationships to their reading and writing. All students need explicit instruction to ensure that they develop this essential learning. Those who start school with less experience of print than others in the class may need more intensive instruction.

Developing concepts about print

Emergent readers and writers of English texts need to acquire a knowledge of the essential conventions of print (that is, the conventions of written text). They learn that:

- print contains a message;
- text is written and read from left to right with a return sweep to the left for the next line;
- there is a one-to-one match between each spoken and written word;
- sentences start with capital letters and end with full stops;
- print on the left-hand page is read before that on the right-hand page;
- the print on a book's cover and title page gives the title and other details, and the cover picture generally suggests what the book is about;
- illustrations convey meaning and relate to the text on the page.

Learning to read and write letters and words

As they learn about letters and words, students need to focus on such aspects as:

- the characteristics of letter formation, including dots, tails, crossbars, and curves;
- differences in letter orientation, such as in "d" and "b";
- the various forms of such letters as "a" (or "ɑ") and "g" (or "ɡ");
- the shape of significant letters, such as the first letter of a child's name;
- upper-case and lower-case forms of letters;
- the shape and length of individual words, such as "hippopotamus" and "book".

Although students may develop much of this knowledge through text-based experiences, teachers will need to teach and reinforce many aspects by explicit instruction. This may occur in a mini-lesson (see page 90) to meet an immediate need that has arisen, but learning should normally occur within a programme of planned reading and writing activities.

In the early stages of reading and writing, children tend to refer to letters in a variety of ways. To provide a consistent identifier, teachers should use the letter names when referring to letters.

Learning about visual-language features of texts

As students learn to recognise various visual-language features of texts, they can apply this knowledge to constructing meaning in their reading and conveying meaning in their writing. Students need to know about:

- the effects of the layout of words, pictures, and captions;
- the way pictures can confirm or convey information;
- the meaning of signs and symbols, such as road signs and logos;
- the significance of the icons on a computer screen;
- the meaning of keyboard symbols, such as arrows.

Electronic forms of text have particular visual-language features. When we read or write electronic forms of text, we draw on our prior knowledge and on the same sources of information as in printed text: syntax, semantics, and grapho-phonic and visual information. However, some conventions and text features are specific to electronic presentation, especially menus, icons, visual symbols, and complex ways of integrating graphics and text. Students need guidance in how to navigate electronic text, just as they do for finding their way through tables of contents, indexes, and other print features when reading or for using them in writing.

Developing a sight vocabulary

It's essential for young readers and writers to develop a sight vocabulary, that is, a store of words that they recognise automatically. At first, students will learn to recognise high-frequency words and personal-interest words.

The development of a sight vocabulary is a key factor in enabling beginning readers to move on.[8] A store of sight words frees the reader from having to process every single word and allows them to work with phrases and sentences. When learners can recognise or write words immediately, they are free to concentrate on meaning as they read or write. Having a store of sight words also helps learners to acquire further sight words. (See the section on page 36 about relating parts of words to sounds.)

However, even the most experienced reader will need to use word-level information at times – for example, when meeting unfamiliar technical terms. And, for beginning readers, reading accurately takes priority over reading fluently. Gradually, with guided practice, they will learn to recognise most words in a text automatically. Learners acquire a vocabulary for reading and writing through:

• reading texts that use high-frequency words repeatedly;

• frequent shared writing sessions where high-frequency words are used repeatedly;

• repeated readings of easy and familiar books;

• writing or dictating their own texts to share with the class and their family, using both familiar and new vocabulary;

• adapting familiar texts in their writing, using similar vocabulary and structures;

• reading and writing notices, labels, notes on the message board, and signs;

• constructing charts of words with common sound or spelling patterns;

• "playing" with words in games, rhymes, and songs.

Relating sounds to print

Children's conversations with adults and with one another are a critical component of literacy learning. Because oral language is such a powerful influence in early literacy development, teachers need to create purposeful opportunities for children to talk.

Emergent readers and writers need to recognise that the stream of sounds they hear in speech is made up of separate words. In written form, there are gaps between the words. Some children will begin to notice these separate words and gaps early, during storybook reading sessions at home or at school. When they see writing modelled at home or at school, and when they write themselves, they consolidate their understanding of words and how they are put together.

By the time children enter … [school, they have generally] gained oral language structures: syntax (structure) and meaning, in particular. In oral language, they have begun to experiment with the sounds language makes. This understanding and knowledge is an important foundation transferred to learning the language of print.

Braunger and Lewis, 1998, pages 16–17

---

[8] Studies reviewed by Pressley (in Block and Pressley, 2002) show a clear link between students' sight vocabulary and their comprehension.

Teachers can develop children's awareness of words, letters, and sounds by drawing attention to these features when reading to them and during shared reading and writing – for example, by focusing on words and phrases that rhyme or have the same first letter or sound. Young children are highly motivated by such activities because they are enjoyable and are often familiar from their early childhood experiences.

Useful activities include:

- reading rhymes and singing songs;
- listening to and practising stories that have repetitive patterns or unusual sounds;
- playing oral word games.

Relating parts of words to sounds

When competent readers meet an unknown word, they tend to break it into sound patterns or look within it for words or word parts that are familiar. Beginner readers usually focus on the initial letter of a word, but it's often useful for them to try to identify parts of the word rather than concentrating on individual letters. Children are often able to work out unknown words by distinguishing between the first part of the word (the onset) and the rest of the word (the rime) as in b-oat, d-og, s-ocks.[9] Once children gain a repertoire of known words, they are better able to recognise familiar patterns in words and can use these patterns to help them solve, pronounce, and write new words. For example, a writer who knows "lunch" is able to work out "munch" by using the spelling pattern that represents the rime "unch". This chunking of information is generally much more successful than trying to sound out a word letter by letter or thinking of one letter at a time when writing. (See also the section on spelling, on pages 144–148.)

Writing and letter-sound relationships

Children's early writing requires them to consider both direction and the details of letters and words that they may not have noticed when they were "reading" texts. As children begin to write, they draw on everything they know about letters and sounds within words (their phonemic awareness and their knowledge of phonics) to match their written words with spoken words. Using approximations in spelling is an important feature of this process.

Children's early writing provides invaluable opportunities for learning about relationships between letters and sounds (phonics). Beginning writers are constantly engaged with the problem of how to write down spoken language – how to represent its sounds and how to spell words. Clearly articulating each sound in a word helps children to make connections between the sounds, the letters, and their own knowledge of spelling patterns.

Children are likely to recognise whole words in speech and reading before they can write them. As they write, they use a variety of methods to attempt unknown words. These include employing phonics (using letters to represent the sounds they hear) and using features such as spelling patterns and regular endings, from words

Share the children's excitement as they make … discoveries and keep your programme flexible enough to build on these learning opportunities. … Children are more likely to make connections between phonics and their reading and writing of texts if they are engaged and involved in making discoveries for themselves.

Sound Sense: Phonics and Phonological Awareness, page 7

The spellings that young children produce are, of course, often incorrect by conventional standards. Using their knowledge of letter names and sounds, children spell the words as they sound to them. And, as shown by their spellings, the children quickly develop an impressive appreciation of the phonemic structure of the English language.

Stahl, Osborn, and Lehr, 1990, page 95

---

[9] For information about rimes in Ready to Read materials and in the Kiwi Kidsongs audio resources, refer to *Sound Sense: Phonics and Phonological Awareness.*

they already know, to help them spell unknown words. This growing knowledge of spelling (orthographic knowledge) contributes greatly to children's fluency in writing.

As they become fluent and experienced readers and writers, children recognise an increasing range of patterns, and they become aware that different letters or letter clusters can represent the same sounds. More sophisticated word study further on involves exploring word families, prefixes, suffixes, and irregular spellings.

Becoming a strategic reader

When we read, we construct meaning by making connections between the text we read and what we already know and can do. Proficient readers at any stage operate in this way. They bring to their reading their knowledge of language and of the world and their knowledge of how to use sources of information in text, and they make sense of the ideas and information in the text accordingly.

Competent readers develop knowledge, a repertoire of strategies, and awareness that enable them to:

- decode, that is, read individual words;
- construct meaning effectively;
- think critically as readers.

Reading for meaning is paramount in school literacy programmes. In order to be able to read for meaning, students need to become accurate and efficient decoders. Through instruction in word identification, teachers ensure that their students become proficient in using visual and grapho-phonic sources of information (see page 30) so that when they encounter an unfamiliar word, they attend to the word itself as a primary source of information. It is important to be explicit when teaching students how to make links between letters (or letter clusters) and their sounds.

Students need to become increasingly fast, automatic decoders of unfamiliar words. In reading, efficient decoding is not an end in itself; it is a means to constructing meaning. Rapid, accurate word recognition frees up the reader's cognitive resources to focus on meaning – not only on surface meanings but also on the deeper messages of a text. The reader then approaches the reading task in a more thoughtful and analytical way and can be encouraged to make their own personal response to the text.

As learners spend more time reading, they encounter commonly used words more often, and these words become familiar to them. Increasingly rapid word recognition has a direct and cumulative effect on a learner's progress. Effective teachers, therefore, provide many, many opportunities for their students to read and write.

Very often, the reader decodes and constructs meaning by drawing on only some of the available information. Children learn to select the best source or sources to focus on. For example, in the sentence "The ducks are going to the river", certain words allow the reader to pay less attention to others. The fact that "ducks" is plural dictates "are". The structure of the English sentence determines the use of "going" and requires a noun at the end of the sentence. These sorts of factors make a text predictable. Children may not be able to explain such rules, but their experience with spoken language means that they come to know them and apply them in their reading and writing. A key role of the teacher is to develop their students' awareness of how to apply and control the rules. (See Developing awareness as a reader and writer, on pages 43–45.)

> The terms *reading strategies* and *processing strategies* are often used interchangeably in the context of learning to read. However, in this book, the term reading strategies has been extended to cover comprehension strategies and the term processing strategies is consistently used to describe the in-the-head ways by which readers make use of the sources of information in text.

Strategies for reading include comprehension strategies as well as processing strategies (which are the in-the-head ways by which readers make use of the sources of information described on pages 28–31). Readers apply the processing strategies in combination with strategies for comprehending and thinking critically about what they read.

Processing strategies

All readers use processing strategies, but they do so at different levels, depending on factors such as the reader's proficiency, the difficulty of the text, and the purpose for reading.

The processing strategies that readers use are:

- *attending* and *searching* – looking purposefully for particular information, known words, familiar text features, patterns of syntax, and information in pictures and diagrams;
- *predicting* – forming expectations or anticipating what will come next by drawing on prior knowledge and experience of language;
- *cross-checking* and *confirming* – checking to ensure that the reading makes sense and fits with all the information already processed;
- *self-correcting* – detecting or suspecting that an error has been made and searching for additional information in order to arrive at the right meaning.

Reading can be thought of as a constantly repeated process of attending and searching, predicting, cross-checking, and confirming or self-correcting. These strategies are not discrete stages; they constantly interact and support one another. They are used in complex combinations, and experienced readers usually apply them automatically. See pages 127–131 in chapter 5 for further detail about teaching students to use processing strategies in the context of text-based experiences.

The ways in which children learn and apply the processing strategies illustrate the importance of metacognition in literacy learning. Beginning readers need to be taught to recognise when to use each strategy; they need to be shown how to apply them deliberately and how to integrate them. Children whose control of the strategies is limited may process text in inappropriate ways – for example, by relying on their memory, by trying to sound out every single word, or by making guesses without appropriate use of the sources of information in the text or their own prior knowledge. Chapter 5 provides examples of how teachers can encourage students to develop metacognition so that they become increasingly able to choose reading strategies for themselves.

Developing comprehension

Comprehension is both a pathway to reading and its end product. Whether we are reading aloud, reading silently, writing, or listening to someone talk, we enter into a mental dialogue with the author, audience, or speaker and explore their ideas or our own in order to make connections. Children begin these explorations when they first set out on their literacy journey, and they continue with further explorations in the instructional settings of classrooms.

Expert readers are active readers who use text and their own knowledge to build a model of meaning, and then constantly revise that model as new information becomes available.

CIERA, 2002, page 1

Comprehension strategies cannot be separated from processing strategies; the teacher's instruction should ensure that their students develop both. Comprehension strategies enable students not only to make sense of the text but also to think about what they are reading. Effective teachers encourage their students to develop strategies that lead to deeper understandings of text.

Comprehension involves:

• getting the message at a basic or literal level, for example, following the plot in a narrative or understanding the facts in a non-fiction text;

• making connections;

• understanding the purpose or intent of a text;

• understanding its form and function;

• responding personally;

• thinking critically about the text.

Learners' comprehension is promoted by:

- having a large oral vocabulary (the implications for rich classroom conversations are discussed further in chapter 4);
- fluency in decoding and a good bank of high-frequency or sight words;
- opportunities to listen actively to the teacher reading aloud;
- extensive reading of a range of texts;
- engagement in many experiences of reading and writing;
- their ability to relate ideas in texts to their background knowledge.

Writing helps to develop comprehension. The discussion involved in, say, shared writing builds students' listening vocabulary and helps them to clarify their ideas. Writers need to attend to the making of meaning – to consider their purpose for writing and how their audience will comprehend what they are writing. Applying this learning helps to develop awareness of how to use comprehension strategies.

... thoughtful, active, proficient readers are metacognitive; they think about their own thinking during reading.
Keene and Zimmerman, 1997, page 22

Comprehension teaching includes both implicit and explicit instruction. In shared reading, for example, the teacher conveys many messages about literacy implicitly as they lead the reading and model what good readers do. Explicit instruction in the context of shared reading often focuses on a particular text feature, such as the use of adjectives to convey a viewpoint. The teacher creates the instructional contexts; the learning may be embedded (implicit), directed (explicit), or both.

Comprehension strategies

Comprehension strategies, like the processing strategies described on pages 38–39, are tools that the reader uses with a purpose in view.

Comprehension strategies may be described as:

- making connections between prior knowledge and the text;
- forming and testing hypotheses about texts;
- asking questions;
- creating mental images, or visualising;
- inferring;
- identifying the author's purpose and point of view;
- identifying and summarising main ideas;
- analysing and synthesising ideas and information;
- evaluating ideas and information.

Like the strategies for processing text, comprehension strategies are not discrete processes to be used one at a time. They are used together: for example, hypothesising involves making connections. They are employed in complex combinations, according to the text itself, the purpose for reading, and the individual learner's pathway of development.

Comprehension strategies are necessary and useful tools for all students – including students who are making rapid progress and need to be extended, those who are struggling to master aspects of literacy learning, and those whose home and community literacy practices differ from the conventional practices in schools. Chapter 4 outlines a number of strategies that teachers can use to help their students to develop these important tools for literacy learning. Chapter 5 describes the comprehension strategies and gives examples of how to engage learners with texts to build their comprehension strategies (see pages 131–135).

Becoming a strategic writer

Like reading, writing involves creating meaning through text. The reader integrates prior knowledge with sources of information in the text to decode and to gain meaning. The writer starts with meaning and integrates prior knowledge and an understanding of how language works to encode and create a text.

Learners need to develop knowledge and a repertoire of strategies for writing across the three aspects of the framework so that they can:

• encode (form words accurately and efficiently);

• create meaning effectively;

• think critically as a writer.

The first of these points can be described as attending to surface features of written text and the second and third as attending to its deeper features.

The sources of information in text that are used for reading are also used when writing. Like readers, writers use semantic, syntactic, and visual and grapho-phonic sources and integrate these with their own prior knowledge and experience to create meaningful text (see pages 30–31).

Just as young readers need to become efficient in decoding, so young writers need to learn to encode effectively – to match sounds to letters in the actual business of writing words. Students need explicit instruction to ensure that they learn to form as well as recognise letters and words rapidly and accurately. They need to master

phonological processing strategies, such as distinguishing the phonemes within words and making accurate links between sounds and letters, and to develop a visual memory for printed words (see pages 32–37).

Students need to build an ever-increasing writing vocabulary (that is, a bank of words that they can write automatically). This frees up the writer's resources to focus on meaning and on other aspects of writing, such as developing an author's perspective and planning the impact on the intended audience. It enables writers to experiment with language and to analyse their work and review it critically.

Students also need to become familiar with the rules of syntax that apply to written English.

Many of the reading comprehension strategies can be related to writing. Good writers, like good readers, synthesise ideas and information. They bring together previous learning and experiences, make connections, visualise, and go on to create imaginative pieces or clear descriptive accounts. They also analyse and evaluate ideas and information as they clarify their intentions, choose vocabulary, begin to compose, and revise their work.

The writing process

The four main stages common to most writing are:

- forming intentions;
- composing a text;
- revising;
- publishing or presenting.

It's important to recognise that these four stages are not discrete but are closely interrelated. The writer does not necessarily move through them in a simple sequence. The writer's movement from one step to the next is influenced by what has gone before and what is anticipated. For example:

- composing and revision are affected by how thoroughly information has been gathered and organised;
- composing often throws up a need for more information;
- decisions made during composing and revising sometimes influence the chosen form of the writing.

The aim of writing instruction is to build students' accuracy, their fluency, and their ability to create meaningful text. The instructional strategies teachers can use to help students achieve this aim are described in chapter 4. Chapter 5 describes the four stages of the writing process in more detail and discusses what it means to engage learners in rich writing experiences. Young writers need many opportunities to practise, to meet new challenges, and simply to enjoy being a writer.

Developing awareness as a reader and writer

The concept of awareness is central to understanding the nature of literacy learning. Students are not always aware of how to use the knowledge and skills they have acquired in literacy activities. Sometimes they may have developed awareness but may not yet be able to put it into words.

Children enter school with varying degrees and kinds of awareness. Some children arrive with a high level of general awareness of written forms of language, some have awareness of certain forms of language, and some may have little awareness of the ways in which they themselves and other people use language. Teachers need to ensure that their instruction and their planning of activities build on the awareness that different children bring.

Children develop social understandings as part of their critical awareness. They need to become aware of the ways in which texts shape values and position audiences. Children can be helped, from the very early stages, to think about what they are reading or writing, for example, to consider an author's choice of language and how it affects the reader.

In order to be able to read and write fluently, students need to develop awareness in each of the three aspects identified in the framework on page 24: learning the code, making meaning, and thinking critically. The kinds of awareness that literacy learners need to develop include:

- print awareness (awareness of the basic conventions of print);
- phonemic awareness (awareness of the separate sounds within words);
- phonological awareness (this more general term describes awareness of the whole sound system of language);
- awareness of the forms and structures of different texts;
- awareness of purpose and perspective in written text;
- awareness of the thinking processes associated with comprehension;
- awareness of ways of using strategies for reading or writing, together with their own prior knowledge, to make meaning.

As students develop their knowledge and strategies, they build awareness of the uses of written language for many purposes. They become aware, for example, that they can use writing to express emotion, to empathise, to argue or persuade - or simply for pleasure. Similarly, they learn that texts can have many purposes and forms and can give great satisfaction and enjoyment. All this enhances students' ability to comprehend and to think critically.

Beginning readers and writers demonstrate their awareness of:

- *sound patterns* when they identify phonemic similarities in rhymes or alliteration;
- *phonics* when they make explicit the relationships between sounds and letters;

Children demonstrate awareness as they attend to new aspects of their world, and their comments from time to time on the printed language around them provide us with good examples of what they are attending to.

Clay, 1998, page 43

43

- *directionality* when they write and read across the page and start again at the left-hand margin;
- *narrative organisation* when they predict what might happen next in a story;
- *features of factual text* when they attend to or use headings or picture captions to build meaning;
- *letter forms and individual words* when they identify details in new text, such as words that begin with the first letter of their own name;
- *syntax* when they apply logical rules to form words within sentences (for example, by ending a present participle with "-ing");
- *chronological sequencing of text* when they use connectives such as "then" and "next" in their writing;
- *language used to convey emotions* when they identify words that express emotions, such as anger or excitement;
- *the use of inference* when they come to a conclusion of their own about a character in a text.

Students develop their awareness through many literacy activities and interactions with the teacher and their peers. Teachers should consciously build learners' awareness by noticing what the learner is attending to and interacting with them to support their learning. An effective teacher knows how to "catch the child in action", as Marie Clay has put it.[10] Chapter 4 discusses some ways of doing this.

Teachers should help their students to identify the knowledge and strategies they use and to deliberately control their use of them. Students do not always develop such awareness automatically. For example, it's necessary to teach students to cross-check when they are reading or writing. Students also need help with what to do when they are "stuck". Handing the responsibility back to the student obliges them to think about what they know and can use and helps them to take increasing responsibility for their own learning (see the examples on page 130 in chapter 5).

Awareness of ways of participating

... children [need] to become aware of the fabric of classroom activities so that they understand the goals and rules of these activities and what is required to perform them.

McNaughton, 2002, page 29

A further kind of awareness is important, especially for children from cultural and linguistic backgrounds with literacy practices that differ from those of the classroom. All learners need to become aware of how they can participate successfully in classroom tasks and activities.[11] The teacher's role is to provide the kind of guidance in literacy activities that enables all students to become aware that:

- an activity has a goal or purpose;
- there are rules about how tasks should be performed;
- there are preferred ways of participating in activities.

In fulfilling this role, the teacher builds on what is familiar to the student and helps the student to become familiar with the established ways of participating in class activities so that they can be comfortable with all that goes on in the classroom.

[10] Clay (1998), page 70

[11] Stuart McNaughton's work has highlighted the importance of developing this awareness. Other relevant studies are by Gee (1998) and Cazden (2001).

Students need to become familiar with the school literacy practices that are associated with success. They also need to become aware of how their own knowledge or ways of doing things can be used in classroom activities.

For students to develop this kind of awareness, their teachers need to know the students and their literacy expertise and to be precise and consistent in their use of instructional language. The teacher should also:

- model and explain, being explicit about what the student needs to do;
- offer many opportunities for focused conversations between student and teacher and among students;
- use consistent language when prompting and questioning, both during an activity and over time.

Teachers need to provide opportunities for their students to apply and practise what they have been taught and to ensure that they all have many and varied enjoyable experiences with rich texts. Activities should be planned to incorporate some elements that are familiar to the student and to include, where necessary, a careful explanation of unfamiliar sections.

Teacher	Can you read me your story? You read me your story.
Mark	(reads his story aloud, pointing to each word) "I see the cat."
Teacher	That's a very good story.
Mark	Cat's outside.
Teacher	Your cat's outside?
Mark	(nods)
Teacher	What does he do while you're at school?
Mark	Having kai.
Teacher	Having kai! Is he? Having kai while you're at school?
Mark	(nods)
Teacher	OK. Can you tell me a story about your cat?
Mark	My cat is (pauses) ... having his kai.
Teacher	All right, then. (Writes "My".) You can write "cat". "My cat ..." Leave a nice big space (indicating where to leave space. Mark writes the letters "ca" and pauses.) Can you hear the sound: "cat ...t ...t"?
Mark	"t"? (Teacher nods. Mark adds the letter "t".)

In this extract from an interaction between a Māori child (who has been at school for several days) and his teacher, Mark is developing awareness of what is expected of him in classroom writing activities. Mark initiates further narrative using a familiar topic. His teacher:

- prompts and encourages with further questioning;
- recognises and accepts Mark's use of a Māori word ("kai"), thus incorporating what is familiar to Mark;
- highlights the last sound in "cat" to clarify what encoding involves.

With the teacher's guidance, Mark is able to add further information and produce a second story. The conversation provides the platform for these developments.

adapted from Turoa, Wolfgramm, Tanielu, and McNaughton, 2002, pages 54–55

Diversity and literacy learning

New Zealand, like many other countries, is seeing a growing diversity among the students in its schools. This is, and will continue to be, a key focus for teachers who face the challenge of providing effective instruction for students in urban areas with culturally and linguistically diverse populations and in other areas where students' achievement levels have been a source of concern. It is crucial that teachers take on board a theory of learning that is based on the concepts of a developmental perspective, the socialisation model, and multiple pathways to successful literacy development (see pages 20–21).

The term *culture* is used in this book to refer to the understandings and formal and informal ways of doing things that a child's family and community share. It does not necessarily relate to ethnicity.

Students come into New Zealand classrooms from many different backgrounds, and teachers need to become aware of what this diversity means for their class programmes and teaching practices. Because every child's literacy learning is grounded in the culture of their family and community, teachers need to gain a knowledge of the literacy practices of local families and to know how language is used in their students' homes.

Some children come from a background of rich oral-language traditions and have a wealth of expertise, for example, in storytelling, to draw upon. Some have experienced family and bedtime story reading; others have developed the practice of transmitting certain kinds of knowledge. Some have learned nursery rhymes; others know and can recite passages of scripture. Many are accustomed to using computers extensively. Some are new learners of English (and even where this is not so, the children in any classroom are likely to use English in a wide range of ways). Some come from family backgrounds where children are not expected to initiate a discussion with an adult, offer an opinion, or comment critically on a text. Some are not in New Zealand by choice, for example, refugee children, who may come with memories of traumatic experiences.

So every child arrives at school with an individual profile of knowledge and skills. Defining this profile can include markers such as alphabet knowledge or concepts about how books work - the conventional assessment of school literacy. It could also include markers from family and community uses of literacy, such as recitation in church.

McNaughton, 2002, page 19

Children from the same cultural, ethnic, or socio-economic group can differ markedly, not only in their achievements but also in the knowledge and experiences that they bring to school literacy practices. Generalisations about groups of students can disadvantage some students or groups.

Such diversity has major implications for teachers' expectations of learners (see chapter 6), their use of instructional strategies and texts (see chapters 4 and 5), and their classroom management and grouping arrangements (see chapter 8).

In a classroom that is a true community of learners, diversity offers tremendous potential for the learning of both the teacher and all the students.

Conclusion

The teacher's role is to provide literacy activities through which their students can develop knowledge and strategies for learning the written code of English, for making meaning, and for thinking critically. The teacher can also develop their students' awareness of how to use their knowledge and strategies in purposeful, enjoyable reading and writing. The teacher should plan for this learning to occur not only during literacy sessions but throughout the school day: literacy is relevant across the curriculum (see also pages 137 and 173).

Teachers need a repertoire of instructional strategies so that they can engage their students in text-based activities that will enable them to progress in their literacy learning. To engage all students effectively, teachers need to have a detailed, dynamic knowledge of the learner – this is the subject of the next chapter.

... the child has the opportunity to understand that skillful strategy use is flexible and always requires thinking, not simply rote applications of rules or knowledge.

Allington, 1997, page 15

Further reading

Texts and reports about literacy acquisition and the need for teachers to have a knowledge about literacy acquisition include:

Braunger, J. and Lewis, J. (1998). *Building a Knowledge Base in Reading.*
Clay, M. M. (1991). *Becoming Literate: The Construction of Inner Control.*
Clay, M. M. (1998). *By Different Paths to Common Outcomes.*
Clay, M. M. (2001). *Change over Time in Children's Literacy Development.*
Luke, A. and Freebody, P. (1999). "A Map of Possible Practices: Further Notes on the Four Resources Model".
McNaughton, S. (1995). *Patterns of Emergent Literacy: Processes of Development and Transition.*
Pressley, M. (2002c). *Reading Instruction That Works: The Case for Balanced Teaching.*
Snow, C. E., Burns, S. M., and Griffin, P., eds (1998). *Preventing Reading Difficulties in Young Children.*
Tunmer, W. E. and Chapman, J. W. (1997). *An Investigation of Language-related and Cognitive-motivational Factors in Beginning Reading Achievement. Final Report Phase I.*

Research and commentary on effective practice for literacy learning in classes with students from diverse cultural and linguistic backgrounds include:

Au, K. H. (1993). *Literacy Instruction in Multicultural Settings.*
Au, K. H. (2002). "Multicultural Factors and the Effective Instruction of Students of Diverse Backgrounds".
Bishop, R. and Glynn, T. (1999). *Culture Counts: Changing Power Relations in Education.*
Bishop, R. and Glynn, T. (2000). "Kaupapa Māori Messages for the Mainstream".
Darling-Hammond, L. (1997). *The Right to Learn: A Blueprint for Creating Schools That Work.*
Dyson, A. H. (1997). *Writing Superheroes: Contemporary Childhood, Popular Culture, and Classroom Literacy.*
Education Review Office (2002). *Māori Students: Schools Making a Difference.*
Hohepa, M. (1993). *Preferred Pedagogies and Language Interactions in te Kōhanga Reo.*
McNaughton, S. (1999). "Developmental Diversity and Beginning Literacy Instruction at School".

For full reference details of the resources listed here, refer to pages 189–194.

McNaughton, S. (2002). *Meeting of Minds.*

Ministry of Education (2003a). *Quality Teaching for Diverse Students in Schooling: Best Evidence Synthesis.*

Nuthall, G. (1999). "Learning How to Learn: The Evolution of Students' Minds through the Social Processes and Culture of the Classroom".

Phillips, G., McNaughton, S., and MacDonald, S. (2000). *Picking up the Pace: Effective Literacy Interventions for Accelerated Progress over the Transition into Decile 1 Schools.*

Tongati'o, L. (1994). *Challenging Success: Developing Pacific Islands Education in Aotearoa, New Zealand.*

Turoa, L., Wolfgramm, E., Tanielu, L., and McNaughton, S. (2002). *Pathways over the Transition to Schools: Studies in Family Literacy Practices and Effective Classroom Contexts for Māori and Pasifika Children.*

Wilkinson, I. A. G. (1998). "Dealing with Diversity: Achievement Gaps in Reading Literacy among New Zealand Students".

Studies and commentary about phonological awareness, phonemic awareness, phonics, and word identification include:

McNaughton, S. (2002). *Meeting of Minds.*

Ministry of Education (1999a). *Literacy Experts Group Report to the Secretary for Education.*

Ministry of Education (2003b). *Ready to Read Teacher Support Material: Sound Sense: Phonics and Phonological Awareness.*

Nicholson, T. and Tan, A. (2002c). "Proficient Word Identification for Comprehension".

Pressley, M. (2002c). *Reading Instruction That Works: The Case for Balanced Teaching.*

Snow, C. E., Burns, S. M., and Griffin, P., eds (1998). *Preventing Reading Difficulties in Young Children.*

Tunmer, W. E. and Chapman, J. W. (1999). "Teaching Strategies for Word Identification".

Tunmer, W. E., Chapman, J. W., Ryan, H. A., and Prochnow, J. E. (1998). "The Importance of Providing Beginning Readers with Explicit Training in Phonological Processing Skills".

The role of motivation in literacy learning is discussed in:

Au, K. H. (2002). "Multicultural Factors and the Effective Instruction of Students of Diverse Backgrounds".

Guthrie, J. T. and Wigfield, A., eds (1999). "Special Issue: How Motivation Fits into a Science of Reading".

Hill, J. and Hawk, K. (2000). *Four Conceptual Clues to Motivating Students: Learning from the Practice of Effective Teachers in Low Decile, Multicultural Schools.*

Texts about the development of comprehension and about effective comprehension instruction include:

Block, C. C. and Pressley, M., eds (2002). *Comprehension Instruction: Research-based Best Practices.*

Braunger, J. and Lewis, J. (1998). *Building a Knowledge Base in Reading.*

CIERA (Center for the Improvement of Early Reading Achievement) (2002). "Improving the Reading Comprehension of America's Children: 10 Research-based Principles".

Duke, N. K. and Pearson, D. (2002). "Effective Practices for Developing Reading Comprehension".

Keene, E. O. and Zimmerman, S. (1997). *Mosaic of Thought: Teaching Comprehension in a Reader's Workshop.*

Pressley, M. (2001). "Comprehension Instruction: What Makes Sense Now, What Might Make Sense Soon".

Pressley, M. (2002b). "Metacognition and Self-regulated Comprehension".

Sweet, A. P. and Snow, C. E. (2003). *Rethinking Reading Comprehension.*

Chapter 3:
Knowledge of the Learner

Introduction

Teachers need an extensive and continually developing knowledge of the learners they teach. Such knowledge encompasses:

- knowing about each learner's pathway of progress;
- knowing about the characteristics of literacy learners in general at different points in their development.

This knowledge informs teachers as they set instructional objectives and learning goals and plan literacy learning activities.

The meaning that is made in any assessment is based not only on what we say and do, but on how we say it and the context and relationship in which it is said. Our assessment interactions with students tell them who we think they are, what we think learners should do, and what we think it means to be literate … Assessments are not simply outcomes, they are part of the process and product of social activity.

Johnston, 1997, page 25

Assessment is a dynamic process that involves gathering, analysing, and using relevant and valid information about the learner. It is informed by teachers' beliefs as well as by their knowledge of literacy learning. Assessment is also a social process and, as such, is an inherent part of literacy programmes, not something that is "done" after the teaching and learning.

Assessment involves identifying the learner's current expertise and deciding on areas for further learning by:

- gathering information in appropriate ways from a range of sources;
- analysing the information;
- making informed judgments about the learner's progress and about how they are achieving in relation to expected outcomes;
- making decisions about future goal setting and instruction;
- using the information to plan for learning activities that will enable the learner to meet the goals and will also lead on to further learning.

Teachers need information about their students' progress in developing literacy knowledge, strategies, and awareness across the three aspects of the literacy framework – learning the code, making meaning, and thinking critically.

Knowledge of learners includes knowledge about the language and literacy practices of their homes and communities. Sometimes teachers may need to find out more about the diverse literacy practices of their students' homes and communities.

Teachers use their knowledge to develop a detailed profile of each student, fitting together many items of information to build as full a picture as possible (see page 65). As the teacher gains new information, they add to or modify the profile.

Effective teachers keep accurate records and keep them up to date by gathering records cumulatively and adding to or modifying them as new data becomes available. Students' personal records of their own progress, while primarily for the students' own benefit, are also a useful source of information for the teacher (see page 62).

Assessment and student outcomes

Many studies show that effective gathering and use of assessment data has a strong influence on students' achievement in literacy learning. Used appropriately, it also has a positive impact on students' motivation and self-esteem. Planned assessment has been found to be a feature of effective literacy teachers' practice.[12]

Assessment leads to improved learning when students are involved in their learning and assessment, receive constructive feedback, and have opportunities to set and achieve their own learning goals. It has also been found that students' learning improves when their teachers modify their practice in the light of assessment data.

Positive outcomes for students from diverse backgrounds have been associated with the gathering and use of assessment data that reflects a detailed knowledge of all students. Studies have also demonstrated the negative effects of inappropriate feedback.

Teachers' value systems and expectations influence the ways that they gather, analyse, and use information about their students. Teachers need to ensure that their own beliefs and assumptions about the potential achievement of particular students or groups of students in their class do not have a negative impact on their selection of assessment procedures or on the way they interpret data.

Assessment can improve the effectiveness of teaching practice. By carefully analysing and using data, teachers can make deliberate adjustments to their teaching in order to meet the revealed needs of their students.

If assessment doesn't make a positive difference to students' learning, then teachers need to consider whether the assessment process is adequate and whether the assessment itself is appropriate and valid. They may also consider whether their instructional strategies need to be modified to meet the students' identified needs.

Assessment can improve teaching and learning when teachers adjust their teaching to take account of the results of assessment.

Ministry of Education, 2003a, page 61

Effective assessment

Characteristics of assessment that promotes learning

Assessment for learning should:[13]

- be part of effective planning of teaching and learning;
- focus on how students learn;

---

[12] Studies that provide this evidence are listed at the end of this chapter.

[13] This list is based on the principles listed in "Assessment for Learning: 10 Principles", Assessment Reform Group (2001).

The single most important element of planning ... is the clarity of learning intentions. Unless teachers are clear about what they want students to learn, it is not possible to develop good assessment of that learning.

Clarke, Timperley, and Hattie, 2003, page 15

- be recognised as central to classroom practice;
- be regarded as a key professional skill for teachers;
- be sensitive and constructive (because any assessment has an emotional impact);
- take account of the importance of learner motivation;
- promote commitment to learning goals and a shared understanding of the criteria for meeting the goals;
- provide learners with constructive guidance about how to improve;
- develop learners' capacity for self-assessment so that they can become reflective and self-managing;
- recognise the full range of achievements of all learners.

General principles of effective assessment

Effective assessment will:

- *focus on process as much as outcomes* – the strategies and knowledge that the students use to solve problems can reveal as much as or more than the results;
- *inform future teaching and learning* by providing understandings and insights and guiding the teacher's practice;
- *be integrated with familiar classroom literacy activities* so that it is a natural part of the day – the students need to be at ease with assessment and see its relevance;
- *allow for student reflection and self-review* – teachers need to ensure that their students understand and articulate both what they have learned and what they need to do to improve further;
- *be culturally appropriate*, taking into account the values and perspectives of all the students;
- *be appropriate socially and emotionally*, promoting the well-being of all the students and affirming their sense of themselves as learners and as members of a learning community (the class).

Being clear about the purpose for assessment

When the teacher has clear instructional objectives, their assessment will be effective because they know what they are looking for. The teacher's purposes for assessment may include:

- finding out what the students already know and what strategies and skills they are using;
- identifying the students' needs in order to plan for timely and focused intervention where appropriate;
- deciding on instructional strategies, approaches, and resource materials to meet the students' needs;
- giving the students constructive feedback and helping them to reflect on their learning.

It is important to distinguish between goal and task. The students need to understand that while the task may be, for example, to compile a recipe, the goal is to learn to write instructions.

The teacher and students have been working on persuasive writing. The shared goal is to write to persuade an audience. The task, in this example, is to write an advertisement for an item that the writer wishes to sell.

The teacher and students jointly developed the following success criteria:
- use words or ideas that will make people want to buy my item;
- describe the features of my item;
- include the price and my contact details.

Robots for Sale.
My robot is for sale, his name is Adim. [Adam]
He can do eny thig you say. You [any]
only have to push a green button to
make It go. And to Stop it you have
to push a red button. It costs $60. I
hope you can bye it. If you want to [buy]
here's the plaS 5 Martin Road. ph
1140560 and Jaite to make
Ghure Lower Hutt.

Room 6   Feedback Form

Name _Rebecca_

Goal _to write to persuade an audience_

FEEDBACK
You've made Adam sound a really smart robot!
You've included cost and contact details – good.

NEXT LEARNING STEPS
You might want to include a 'wow' thing your robot can do.
Check the spelling of the underlined words.

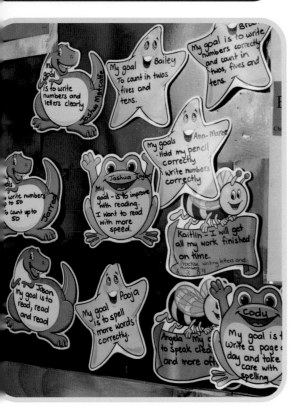

Assessment and feedback

Effective assessment provides the student with feedback to enhance their learning. Feedback on learning is embedded in everyday classroom interactions and in teacher planning, and it is most effective when the teacher has in-depth knowledge of the students. Feedback as a tool for literacy teaching is discussed in chapter 4. In the context of assessment, effective feedback:

- begins with positive comments about the learner's work;
- is specific to the intended outcome and the shared goal for the task;
- is always directed towards the intended outcome, not the learner;
- is primarily descriptive rather than evaluative;
- is offered as soon as possible after the task has been carried out;
- offers the learner guidance on the next steps in their learning;
- invites the learner's suggestions about what they could do to improve their learning.

The teacher needs to allow time for the students to discuss and act on the feedback in order to reinforce their understanding of how they can use it to improve their learning.

Gathering information

General principles for information gathering

When gathering information, it is important that:

- the teacher is clear about their instructional objectives;
- the teacher is clear about the learning goals (the intended outcomes for the students);
- the teacher is clear about what information is to be gathered and why;
- information is gathered from many sources;
- the teacher selects appropriate procedures and administers them appropriately;
- all those who gather and use the data understand its strengths and limitations (that is, what information it does and does not provide);
- the data gathering is well managed.

The data used must be rigorous. For example, opportunities for students to read and write have been associated with success in literacy learning. However, data that records students being given such opportunities (time for silent reading or independent writing, logs of the number of books read or items written) does not, in itself, provide evidence of gains in literacy learning.

A range of sources

A range of sources can be used to gather information about a student's literacy learning, both formally and in informal settings. These sources include:

- the student (as an individual, as one of a group of peers, or when working with the teacher);
- the student's family and community;
- other partners in the student's learning, such as specialist support staff.

A range of assessment procedures

Assessment procedures are ways of gathering information. Through well-chosen assessment procedures, teachers can gather information about students' development of knowledge, strategies, and awareness. Whether their students are decoding and encoding, building meaning as they read or creating meaning as they write, or responding critically to what they read and write, teachers need to plan to use appropriate assessment procedures. The various procedures are described briefly below.[14]

Observation-based procedures

The value of the teacher's observation of students and their learning is often underestimated.

Informal observation

A great deal of information gathering occurs naturally during the everyday activities of the classroom. Informal and anecdotal information can have tremendous value. Teachers have opportunities, every time they observe a student, to review and add to their existing knowledge of that learner and to use this knowledge to inform their decisions about the next steps for that student's learning. Teachers can gather a lot of useful knowledge about a student's social and emotional strengths as well as their literacy learning, for example, by:

- observing what the student does when they can choose a literacy activity and how they work when they are alone;
- listening to their conversations with their peers;
- noting how they receive and act on feedback.

Studies have shown that one of the characteristics of effective teachers is great skill in using informal observations to inform their professional judgments. Such teachers are likely to use formal procedures to confirm or clarify information they have gained from observations rather than to identify learning needs.

Through systematic observation, effective teachers get to know their children very well, well enough to provide to the children feedback that matches their level of understanding, informing them and motivating them to progress their achievement – in other words, personalised instruction.

Keith, 2002, page 12
(summarising Phillips,
McNaughton, and
MacDonald, 2000)

---

[14] *Guided Reading: Years 1–4* includes, on pages 22–24, ideas for gathering information about literacy learners in the context of guided reading.

Structured observations focusing on a goal

Structured observations of individuals or small groups can be scheduled at any time during classroom activities. The teacher consciously plans to observe how the students set about tasks or how they use specific literacy strategies. Structured observations are characterised by a clear assessment focus, although the teacher usually gathers incidental information at the same time.

Structured observation of new entrants is especially important, given the wide range of knowledge and expertise that children bring at school entry (see pages 20-21).

When observing an emergent reader or writer, the teacher may choose to focus on any one of the following questions that is relevant to that child's learning pathway.

- Is this child using appropriate sources of information to solve or write new words?
- Is this child trying to make meaning when they read and write?
- Is this child attending appropriately to details of print when reading and writing?
- Does this child choose to read and write independently?
- Is this child confident in reading to others or sharing ideas with them?

Teachers characteristically keep a great deal of information in their heads, but it's important to jot down and date notes during observations. Notes about significant details of what learners are attending to when they read or write are especially useful. These notes, in conjunction with other information and the teacher's professional judgment, contribute to decisions about a learner's next steps. Often the teacher will see patterns developing in their notes on a student and will schedule a formal assessment or a conference with the student.

Systematic, structured, and recorded observations help to ensure that the teacher gives equitable attention to the needs of all learners in the class - those making rapid progress as well as those not making the expected progress.

Conversations, conferences, and interviews

Interviews and conversations with a student are very valuable because they give the teacher opportunities to build their knowledge of that learner by:

- gathering information about the student's progress and discussing this with the student;
- clarifying the strategies the student is using and ensuring that the student is becoming aware of how to control these strategies;
- learning about the student's personal interests and their attitudes to learning;
- identifying and discussing problems or obstacles to learning that the teacher may not have been aware of;
- providing personalised, specific feedback;
- agreeing on goals for further learning.

Such conversations are most effective when they focus on the purpose for the learning and on shared success criteria. Chapter 4 contains a discussion (on pages 88–89) about the value of classroom conversations for children's learning.

It's a real challenge to plan time with individual students during the busy classroom day. However, the effort is worthwhile because the teacher gains an in-depth knowledge of the learner, and the student gains further understandings and motivation to learn. Conferences or interviews can be held with individuals or with small groups.

Careful prompting will help a student to keep an active role. This is important because, when the teacher dominates the discussion, the student's ability to express themselves can be inhibited, and the teacher may wrongly assume that the student has less or more knowledge or expertise than they actually have.

Classroom conversations can be informal and spontaneous, for example, when the teacher moves alongside a student and strikes up a conversation about the work they are doing. The teacher should have a focus and seek to gain more knowledge of that learner.

… asking questions is not the only way to get information. Giving information can frequently be a better way. For example, to respond to a student's writing with your sincere reaction to it ("The part in the middle about the horse made me feel very sad, but I felt a bit confused about the part where you were going home") can have a more productive effect than asking direct questions ("Why did you write the part about going home in that way?") or making assertions ("This is badly written"). The personal response at once gives a reason for clarification and shows respect for the writer and the piece of writing without necessarily invoking a power differential.

Johnston, 1997, page 22

Conferences with parents and other partners in each student's learning will add to the teacher's store of information about the student and help to build a fuller picture of that student as a learner. Again, these conversations will be most effective when they focus on the intended outcomes for the student's learning. (Refer to chapter 7 for more information on partnerships.)

In this example, the teacher interacts with a year 3 student, a fairly confident reader who is just starting to read simple chapter books.

Teacher	Tell me about how you choose library books.
Student	I get the smiley face ones.
Teacher	How do you know which smiley face books to choose?
Student	The cover, and sometimes I know about them cos other kids have talked about them.
Teacher	You could look at the blurb on the back, too. That tells you a lot about the book.
Student	Oh, yes, I do that sometimes.
Teacher	Do you read the books yourself?
Student	Sometimes I get Mum and Dad to read bits, and sometimes I read them myself.
Teacher	The five finger test could help you to see how hard a book might be, so you know whether you can read it yourself. Remember how to do that?
Student	Oh, yeah.
Teacher	Tell me about the book you're reading now.
Student	It's about soccer.
Teacher	What do you think of it?
Student	It's good. It's about a big match – and I can read it myself!
Teacher	Great.

Standardised assessment procedures

Standardised diagnostic assessment procedures include the School Entry Assessment procedure, the running records procedure, and the Observation Survey or six-year net. Other standardised procedures are the tasks in the Assessment Resource Banks and the New Zealand Council for Educational Research's Progressive Achievement Tests (PAT).

School Entry Assessment

This set of three specific procedures is designed specifically for use with children starting school. It enables teachers of new entrants to gather information about their literacy and numeracy skills and to confirm or review impressions gained during the first two or three weeks and so make informed decisions when planning the child's programme.[15] The tasks of School Entry Assessment include a retelling task, a "concepts about print" task, and a task focusing on numeracy skills.[16]

Running records

The running records procedure provides a framework for systematically observing a child's reading behaviour. This procedure, developed by Marie Clay, employs standard methods with recognised conventions for recording exactly what the child does as they read. Through careful observation, reliable scoring, and thoughtful interpretation, the teacher gains significant insights into the child's:

- strategies for solving unknown words;
- competence in drawing together all the sources of information;
- self-monitoring and self-correction strategies;
- willingness to take risks.

In addition to the core procedure, the teacher may explore the child's comprehension of the text by inviting the child to retell the story or by asking questions that require them to interpret what they have read. (These, however, are not part of the running records procedure.)

Taking running records regularly is an essential part of teachers' planned, targeted monitoring to ensure that the students' learning needs are met. Running records are of particular strategic use with students in the early years who may be at risk of not making the expected progress in reading. Running records are also useful for students at any level who are not making the expected progress in reading.[17]

---

[15] The Ministry of Education resource *SEA: School Entry Assessment*, which is based on extensive research on the reliable assessment of young children, is available to all schools with year 1 to 4 classes.

[16] The same range of tasks has also been developed in te reo Māori. *AKA: Aro matawai Urunga-ā-Kura* is used with children entering a programme where the language of instruction is Māori.

[17] The Ministry of Education video resource kit *Using Running Records*, which is in all schools with year 1 to 3 classes, provides full details of the procedure for taking running records, interpreting them, and using the results for further teaching. The Kia Ata Mai Educational Trust can provide a form of running record assessment for the Māori language.

The Observation Survey

The Observation Survey developed by Marie Clay[18] provides six measures for systematically observing children who have been at school for a year. The tasks cover oral language, concepts about print, reading of continuous text, letter knowledge, reading vocabulary, writing vocabulary, and hearing and recording sounds in words. Because of its detailed attention to specific essential skills, this survey is especially helpful in identifying children who appear to be making uneven progress.[19]

Assessment Resource Banks

The Assessment Resource Banks are an online collection of assessment materials. Resources are available for English (as well as maths and science) to assess achievement in relation to the New Zealand Curriculum at levels 2 to 5.

These tasks include a number designed for criteria-referenced observation. The Assessment Resource Banks can be accessed online (see page 189).

Progressive Achievement Tests

The main series of standardised tests for New Zealand literacy learners are those developed by the New Zealand Council for Educational Research. The range includes the Progressive Achievement Test (PAT) series, which schools can use to assess listening comprehension from year 3 and reading vocabulary, reading comprehension, and information skills from year 4 (see page 193). These tests are administered and marked to specified standards.

Other standardised tests

Teachers of students in years 3 to 4 may also use the asTTle CD-ROM[20] of assessment tools for literacy and numeracy (curriculum levels 2 to 4) and the Supplementary Tests of Achievement in Reading (STAR),[21] available from the New Zealand Council for Educational Research.

The folder *English for Speakers of Other Languages: Information for Schools* (Ministry of Education, 2002a) includes materials that teachers of students from non-English-speaking backgrounds can use to assess these students.[22]

---

[18] Clay (2002)

[19] A reconstruction, by Clay and Rau (1998), can be used where the language of instruction is Māori.

[20] Ministry of Education and the University of Auckland (2003).

[21] Elley (2000)

[22] This folder is available from the Ministry of Education National ESOL Literacy Team.

Non-standardised assessment tasks

These are informal tools, usually developed by teachers and other educators regionally, which may be in common use but are not standardised. Two tools that are commonly used to assess students' reading are informal prose inventories and cloze tests.

Informal prose inventories

Informal prose inventories are selections of different types of text with each text presented (usually) in two sections. The student reads the first section aloud while the teacher takes a running record to establish the student's accuracy, and then they complete the reading silently. The teacher then uses questions and discussion to explore the student's understanding of what they have read.

Because an informal prose inventory involves both oral and silent reading, the teacher can gather a wide range of information, including information about the learner's use of word-level information and their comprehension (for example, about whether they are inferring and making connections).

Cloze tests

The cloze procedure is used to assess students' reading comprehension. Students are required to use clues from the context or surrounding text to help them identify words that have been deliberately removed from the text. If students can successfully fill in the blanks, they are probably able to comprehend that text when reading independently.

Using information from a student's writing

A student's writing gives a clear indication of their grasp of vocabulary and sentence patterns, of the range and depth of their ideas, and of how well they understand purpose and audience in writing. Their writing also conveys information about their emotional and cultural engagement in the writing task. It is a uniquely valuable source of information for the teacher.

Refer to page 66 for information about the New Zealand curriculum exemplars for English, which provide details about the kinds of information that can be gathered from a student's writing.

Self-assessment and peer assessment

Information from students' self-assessment

Good readers and writers are constantly monitoring their own reading and writing as they work. As part of becoming aware of how to use knowledge and strategies, they learn to give themselves feedback (self-generated feedback). Teachers need to help their students to develop the habit of monitoring and assessing themselves. It is useful to develop with the students a set of shared success criteria for a particular task. Students' records and views of their own progress provide teachers with a source of further knowledge of these learners.

Students' self-assessment yields highly valuable knowledge for the teacher. The students' own comments on and interpretations of their learning and problem solving can reveal to teachers what their students are thinking in terms of:

- what they have learned;
- what they understand;
- what else they need to know;
- what thoughts they have on their next learning steps.

Self-assessment enables students to set appropriate personal learning goals and can also help motivate them to learn. It's useful to negotiate with the students a framework for reflection. Such a framework should encourage depth of thinking and provide a good model for self-analysis. Both the process and the outcome of the student's self-assessment add to the information that the teacher takes into account in assessing their progress.

A framework that students could use for self-assessment against a shared goal

Two things I like about my work are ...

I want to know more about ...

Something new I've learned is ...

I had a problem with ...
    but I worked it out by ...

One thing I need to work on is ...

I would like to tell my buddy ...

Information from peer assessment

Peer assessment, in a supportive classroom environment that is a community of learners, can yield valuable information for both teacher and students. The students can comment on and analyse one another's work. For example, in a writing task, they could give feedback on a peer's treatment of topic, text organisation, fluency, word choice, or author's voice, using the same criteria that they had applied to their own work. As the teacher supports and observes the peer assessments, they build their knowledge of all the students involved.

Selecting assessment procedures

When deciding on procedures for gathering data, it's best not to assume that certain procedures should always be used. Teachers should be prepared to ask, as a starting point, "What do I want to know, and how can I best find out?"

Consider which of the possible procedures are:

- most suitable for the purpose;
- most suitable from the perspective of the learners' cultures, including their first languages and their home literacy practices.

Consider, too, the way the data is gathered. Conventional ways may not best meet the purpose of the assessment or reveal all the expertise that children bring to the classroom.[23]

Administering assessment procedures

Assessment is likely to be most effective where the relationship between teacher and student is one of trust and mutual respect and when teacher and student have shared understandings and expectations about the student's learning. It's important to be sensitive and constructive when giving feedback and to ensure the comfort, safety, and general well-being of the student who is being assessed. The physical relationship of the learner and the assessor conveys many messages; for example, they can sit side by side rather than opposite each other.

Different behaviours can influence the results of an assessment. For example, an assessor may not allow adequate "wait time" or may misinterpret a child's silence.

---

[23] Refer to www.tki.org.nz/r/assessment/two/pdf/reviews.pdf
for a web page on the strengths and weaknesses of assessment tools.

Analysing information

General principles for analysing information

There are general principles for analysing data and reflecting on it.

- The analysis is based on the teacher's current knowledge of the learners.
- The reliability and validity of the data have been established.
- The teacher understands the strengths and limitations of the procedure and of the data.
- The analysis takes account of qualitative influences on the students' performance, such as the effect of people's expectations.
- The teacher recognises that the information to be analysed is dynamic in nature (because students and their learning constantly change and move on).
- Judgments can be checked and confirmed because they are based on the analysis of information from many sources, not one isolated source.
- The student's own assessment of their learning is considered and valued.

All assessment occurs in a particular time and place and involves a specific task. When analysing assessment information, the teacher needs to be aware of the context in which the information was gained. In any assessment activity, many factors may affect the outcomes. For example, when a student finds the structure of the task familiar and interesting, that student will engage with the task more readily.

Developing a full picture of any learner means fitting the pieces together. This is especially important where the students come from backgrounds with literacy practices that differ from the school's. Where this is so, the teacher will need to analyse and reflect on information gathered not only in classroom literacy activities but also in various other settings (for example, in intervention programmes, homes, and communities) and across the curriculum.

Collegial analysis of assessment information by two or more teachers is very valuable. The process of talking through the implications of the evidence helps teachers to clarify what achievements they are looking for and to establish a sound basis for their judgments.

At all times, an effective evaluator of information is prepared to be surprised. Teachers should always be ready to assume that a student may know more, and be able to do more, than previous assessment information has shown.

Analysis for varying purposes

Information, whether about the whole school, a group within the school, one class, a group within a class, or an individual, may be analysed for different purposes. For example, analysis can be used to:

- describe students' current literacy-related knowledge, strategies, and awareness in relation to agreed expectations;
- examine the relationships between students' current literacy levels and general patterns of progress in literacy acquisition (see pages 70–74);
- describe students' progress in relation to other known patterns of development or nationwide data.

For their immediate classroom purposes, teachers often focus on analysing information from one source, for example, by:

- taking a running record and analysing the student's use of processing strategies in order to gain information about their learning needs;
- noting the features of a student's writing in a specified writing task and promptly following up with feedback and suggestions for the next steps;
- identifying a problem in spelling and addressing it immediately;
- identifying or clarifying the learner's view of their own learning.

For a valid assessment of a student's progress over time, however, the teacher needs to make a more considered analysis of a collection of information from more than one source.

Using cumulative files or portfolios

Many teachers assemble a cumulative file or portfolio of each student's work (especially their writing) to use as a source of information to analyse.

Work samples offer tangible evidence of students' development. Teachers gather drafts as well as finished writing in different forms so that they can reflect on the processes the writer used.

Other useful information for the file includes running records and the teacher's notes from observations and interviews. Evidence of students' developing metacognition and of their critical awareness in reading and writing is particularly valuable. Students' book reports and reading logs help the teacher to build a detailed profile. This range of information enables the teacher to monitor their students' learning and provide them with feedback to guide their pathways of progress over time. Portfolios have a useful role in student self-assessment. When the teacher and student discuss a portfolio in a reflective way, this adds depth to their joint knowledge of the student's progress and clarifies, for both of them, the next learning steps.

The portfolio should be a positive record of progress that both teacher and student can feel proud to share with peers, family, and other partners in the student's learning.

Using exemplars

The New Zealand Curriculum Exemplars are examples of students' work that are annotated to illustrate learning, achievement, and quality in relation to curriculum level. There are writing exemplars for levels 1 to 5 (as well as exemplars for oral language and visual language). Exemplars help to answer the question "What do we mean by 'quality work'?" They provide reference points that help teachers and students to make decisions about the students' current achievement and progress and about the next steps for teaching and learning. The New Zealand curriculum exemplars can be accessed online (the website reference is on page 192).

Teachers can develop school-based exemplars by assessing work samples collegially. This helps the school to develop shared understandings of criteria and shared language to describe students' work. Considering school-based exemplars alongside the New Zealand curriculum exemplars for English is a valuable exercise.

Useful focuses for analysis

There are many ways in which teachers can build their knowledge of their students. They may analyse the information they have gathered in order to:

- compare various aspects of a student's work to identify any inconsistencies in their progress and to note how they perform with different types of tasks and in different contexts;

> Does the student work effectively in a group? Was the student's interest a strong factor affecting their success in reading or writing a particular text? Is their enthusiasm matched by accuracy?

- focus on a student's particular learning need (for example, a need to gain the confidence to write independently) and consider what the assessment evidence suggests in terms of that student's interests, use of strategies, and choice of topic;
- consider a series of results for the same student from the same procedure (for example, running records taken over several months) and assess the student's progress towards independence (for example, as shown by their beginning to apply their strategies to more complex texts);
- compare the data from different students working towards the same learning outcome;

> Is there a common pattern of strengths and weaknesses? Do the results have implications for the instructional programme, for grouping, or for extension work for some students?

- document evidence of a student's progress not only in learning the written code of English and making sense of it but also in developing critical awareness;

> How rich is the student's written vocabulary? Can the student make inferences? Can they discuss the author's perspective in a book report?

- consider the achievement of identified target groups of students and decide whether the teacher's instruction needs to change in order to help them achieve better outcomes or whether an intervention programme would be more effective;
- reflect on the effectiveness of their teaching.

Part of the professionalism of teachers is their readiness to consider whether their own instructional practice may need to change. They may, as a result of analysing data, reflect on and monitor their use of the deliberate acts of teaching described on pages 78–87 (for example, their use of questions or feedback) or their effectiveness in generating classroom conversations.

As a result of teachers' analysis and reflection, they go on to set new objectives for their students' literacy learning – and for their own practice.

Using assessment information

General principles for using assessment information

When using assessment information, the teacher:

- bases their use of assessment data on their knowledge of literacy learning;
- creates opportunities to use the information through planned literacy activities (timed to have the most beneficial effect on the students' learning);
- selects instructional strategies and text-based activities purposefully, as a result of analysis and the objectives arising from the analysis;
- plans feedback to students to inform and guide them and also as a basis for shared goal setting;
- is critically reflective about their teaching practice and modifies it as necessary.

Using assessment information to inform teaching practice

Teachers need to be strategic and deliberate in taking action on the basis of what assessment information tells them. The quality of their planning for the deliberate use of instructional strategies and literacy activities reflects the quality of the information they have gathered and analysed. Teachers who know that their decisions are based on high-quality information are confident and focused in their practice.

It is crucial that students take part in setting goals for their own learning and have clear strategies for achieving their goals. In order to help all their students to set appropriate goals, teachers need a detailed and dynamic knowledge of each student's progress in using the written code, making meaning, and developing critical awareness.

Teachers who gather and analyse data effectively are also better able to engage their students in text-based activities.

These extracts show a teacher's analysis and use of assessment information to decide what to do next for the student's learning.

Jonah (reading at Blue 2)
26 March
On running record, only 90% accuracy and SC 1:9. Uses visual information (mostly initial letters) quite well but isn't rereading to cross-check the meaning against the visual. Sometimes rereads but isn't checking that the rereading makes sense!

I need to stand back more and get him to make the decisions, e.g., "Does that sound right to you?" "Does that make sense?" (even if it does! I don't want him to get too reliant on me pointing out errors). I'll have a word with his mum too about her not helping too much and about passing responsibility back to Jonah.

7 April (still Blue 2)
96% accuracy and SC 1:4 — big improvement! (Mum has noticed the difference, too.) He's often stopping and working out what to do when he detects an error. Can explain what he is doing when cross-checking. Uses prediction well. But needs lots of practice — his strategy use is still not completely secure. He pauses and thinks more about what he's reading now that he's not totally focused on decoding, and he comments on the text — I'll encourage this during discussion in guided reading. Check whether he's ready for Blue 3 after the holidays.

When they have analysed their assessment information, teachers can use it to:

- consider the progress of individual students and identify their needs to determine how to extend and support their literacy development;
- group students for learning activities;

- plan the activities and approaches that will best support the students;
- make informed choices of resource materials;
- reflect on their own teaching practice;
- review their literacy programme and modify the daily and weekly schedule;
- review their classroom organisation and management;
- make the best use of teacher-aide time, specialist services, volunteer help, and peer or buddy support.

Sharing assessment information with students can be a powerful way to:

- keep them motivated (because they see the evidence of their progress);
- affirm and make explicit what they can do;
- enable them to set specific goals for further learning.

When students' goals are set as a result of shared assessment information, both teacher and students can consciously use the information to improve learning.

Using assessment information to build partnerships

Assessment information enables the teacher and the school to build partnerships with the students' parents and families. For example, they may:

- share with families descriptions of their children's progress that are based on accurate and current information (these descriptions can be specific about what the student can do);
- work with families to develop and discuss shared expectations for the students' learning and to set shared goals that all understand.

It is also important for teachers and other stakeholders in the students' learning to share assessment information and to ensure that they all have consistent expectations about the students' progress. (See chapter 7.)

Using assessment information across the whole school

Assessment information can be used for school improvement. For example, schools can use it to:

- analyse trends and set new goals across the school and for all year groups;
- identify individuals or groups of students who are at risk of not achieving to their potential and plan appropriate action;
- consider the implications of assessment information for the school's organisation and practices;
- set whole-school goals for improvement in resources or in identified areas of the curriculum;
- plan professional development for teachers that relates to identified goals for student achievement;
- meet the school's reporting requirements.

Effective teachers actively involve students in their own learning and assessment, make learning outcomes transparent to students, offer specific, constructive, and regular feedback, and ensure that assessment practices impact positively on students' motivation.

Ministry of Education, 2003a, page 61

Patterns of progress

The following indicators for reading and writing summarise what literacy learners may be expected to know and be able to do after one year of literacy instruction and after four years. The indicators are based on the teaching and learning systems, programmes, and curriculum documents that are currently in place in New Zealand schools.

It's important that the patterns of progress reflected in these indicators are seen as negotiable and dynamic, not as fixed end points or "stages". Within this general pattern, there are variations both in how children progress and in the rate at which they progress. However, it is important to know about the general patterns of progress – they shape our expectations for individual children's progress and achievement. The ultimate goal is to raise the achievement of all students, not to bring as many students as possible to some arbitrary, "average" level of performance at any point in their progress through school. The indicators support teachers by providing a guide for setting instructional objectives and learning goals.

Patterns at school entry

When children start school, they bring a range of knowledge, understandings, and behaviours. The following information from the "competent children" research[24] gives an idea of the behaviours that one group of children exhibited at age five.

Parents reported that their children:

- could look at books by themselves (94 percent);
- could write or pretend to write their names (94 percent);
- could memorise stories (86 percent).

Researchers found that children:

- could handle books appropriately (87 percent);
- understood that the text rather than the picture is to be read (61 percent);
- could turn the pages one at a time and could retell a story relating to the pictures (81 percent);
- could locate a word (51 percent);
- could identify the first letter of their name (85 percent);
- could give another word starting with that letter (69 percent);
- could identify the sound relating to that letter (45 percent);
- could write their name spontaneously and correctly (46 percent).

They found that the majority of the children were confident in communicating with others and could solve problems in their exploration, games, and construction activities.

---

[24] For this research, refer to Wylie and Else (1998) and to Wylie, Thompson, and Lythe (1999 and 2001).

Indicators

At the end of year 1

Reading and writing: end of year 1

- Has a positive attitude to reading and writing
- Is aware of the sound systems of English and can apply this awareness to their reading and writing
- Can identify and distinguish many individual sounds within words and can apply this knowledge to their reading and writing
- Is curious about language – its vocabulary, idioms, grammar, style, and changes over time
- Is beginning to understand that reading and writing can be for a range of purposes.

Reading: end of year 1

- Understands that we read to get meaning
- One-to-one matching, directionality, and return sweep well established
- Letter-sound relationships secure for all single letters and for some consonant digraphs and consonant blends
- Can sound out simple, decodable words in text
- Has a large and increasing bank of automatically recognised high-frequency words[25]
- Uses the sources of information in text (meaning, structure, and visual and grapho-phonic information) and prior knowledge to make sense of what they read
- Uses processing strategies, such as predicting and self-correction, with increasing confidence and also self-monitors
- Understands the purposes of some punctuation features
- Confidently approaches challenges in their reading and will persevere when having difficulty
- Can use phrasing, intonation, and emphasis to read expressively
- Uses appropriate language about books, for example, the terms title, author, illustration, and cover
- Is able to comprehend texts and to think and talk critically about the ideas and language in them
- Is able to distinguish some different text forms, for example, letters, stories, and instructions.

There is a widely held expectation among teachers that children at the end of year 1 will be reading at (or beyond) Blue to Green levels on the Ready to Read colour wheel.[26]

---

[25] Refer to the Ready to Read lists on TKI at www.tki.org.nz/r/literacy_numeracy/professional/teachers_notes/ready_to_read/rr_level_search_e.php

[26] Refer to *Reading and Beyond* for information about the Ready to Read colour wheel and to the *Ready to Read Teacher Support Material* for ideas for using the series with students.

Writing: end of year 1

- Understands that we write to communicate ideas, information, and feelings
- Can hear and record most of the dominant sounds in words
- Can write some high-frequency words
- Shows awareness of print conventions and uses some punctuation features
- Leaves spaces between words
- Displays a strong sense of directionality
- Is able to write simple ideas, reasons, opinions, and responses, often around personal experience
- Can organise ideas and plan writing, for example, by using talk, pictures, or brainstorming to develop ideas
- Is confident about writing on a range of topics
- Is aware of an audience for their writing and is able to gain some audience interest
- Is beginning to develop a personal voice in their writing
- Can write simple sentences
- Can write more than one sentence in a writing session
- Is beginning to use a variety of sentence structures
- Attempts to use topic-specific vocabulary
- Is willing to take risks in spelling
- Knows where to find information to support their spelling
- Can read what they have written and talk about it
- With support, can talk and make suggestions about other writers' work
- With support, can respond to feedback and make changes to their writing, for example, by adding detail or correcting surface features
- Is developing the ability to think critically about their work and reflect on its quality.

At the end of year 4

Reading and writing: end of year 4

- Has a positive attitude to reading and writing and is enthusiastic about reading and writing a wide range of texts
- Reads and writes for enjoyment and to gain and provide information
- Chooses to write and read independently for different purposes
- Has a wide vocabulary of written English and is continually expanding their personal bank of words and terms
- Uses dictionaries and a variety of other reference tools
- Can recognise and discuss the features and purposes of different text forms
- Is reflective about their own reading and writing; monitors and self-evaluates
- Expects to receive and act on feedback from others to improve their reading and writing.

Reading: end of year 4

- Integrates meaning, structure, visual and grapho-phonic information, and prior knowledge when reading
- Selects and uses the processing strategies effectively and self-monitors
- Uses word-identification strategies appropriately and automatically when encountering unknown words
- Can confidently share and discuss their thoughts about and responses to a range of texts – fiction and non-fiction, print texts and electronic texts
- Thinks critically about what is being read
- Can use a range of comprehension strategies: can analyse and interpret what the author is saying, make inferences and justify them, and make connections
- Can gather, process, and evaluate information from a variety of sources, including multimedia sources
- Usually reads silently
- Can read aloud with expression and fluency
- Demonstrates a developing understanding of text structure and author's style when discussing texts
- Has a strong sense of what they like to read and can locate such material.

There is an expectation among teachers that children at the end of year 4 will be able to read, comprehend, and respond to texts that are widely agreed to be appropriate at their chronological age.

Writing: end of year 4

- Can confidently express ideas and opinions and describe personal experiences
- Can write on a range of topics
- Plans and organises ideas and information logically
- Shows awareness of audience and purpose through choice of content, language, and text type
- Conveys a personal voice where appropriate
- Responds to feedback and can modify writing
- Is able to vary sentence structures and lengths
- Uses varied and precise verbs, adjectives, and adverbs to convey ideas and uses simple conjunctions to link ideas
- Is able to use language structures and features for impact, for example, varied sentence structures, similes, and rich vocabulary
- Uses print conventions and punctuation confidently to support meaning
- Uses knowledge of consonant and vowel sounds, of common spelling patterns, and of word derivations to encode words
- Spells most high-frequency words correctly
- Independently checks for spelling and presentation

There is information on TKI about deeper and surface features of writing, as identified in *The New Zealand Curriculum Exemplars*, at www.tki.org.nz/r/assessment/exemplars/eng/matrices/matrx_pi_about_e.php

- Is able to use a variety of reference tools
- Uses information gained in reading to inform their writing
- Thinks critically about their writing and evaluates it according to success criteria
- Is able to analyse and discuss the writing of others
- Is developing the ability to revise their writing to suit the purpose and to clarify its meaning and add to its impact
- Can publish and present in a range of media.

Further reading

For full reference details of the resources listed here, refer to pages 189–194.

Research that links effective assessment with student achievement is summarised in:
Ministry of Education (2003a). *Quality Teaching for Diverse Students in Schooling: Best Evidence Synthesis.*

Texts that discuss the nature and practice of assessment and how effective use of assessment information impacts on achievement include:
Black, P. and Wiliam, D. (1998a). "Assessment and Classroom Learning".
Black, P. and Wiliam, D. (1998b). *Inside the Black Box: Raising Standards through Classroom Assessment.*
Clarke, S., Timperley, H., and Hattie, J. (2003). *Unlocking Formative Assessment: Practical Strategies for Enhancing Students' Learning in the Primary and Intermediate Classroom.*
Crooks, T. J. (1988). "The Impact of Classroom Evaluation Practices on Students".
Hattie, John (1999). "Influences on Student Learning".
Johnston, P. H. (1997). *Knowing Literacy: Constructive Literacy Assessment.*
Sadler, D. R. (1989). "Formative Assessment and the Design of Instructional Systems".
Wilkinson, I. A. G. (1998). "Dealing with Diversity: Achievement Gaps in Reading Literacy among New Zealand Students".

Further useful resources on assessment include:
Askew, S., ed. (2000). *Feedback for Learning.*
Assessment Reform Group (2001). "Assessment for Learning: 10 Principles: Research-based Principles to Guide Classroom Practice".
Clay, M. M. (2002). *An Observation Survey of Early Literacy Achievement.*

Information and comment gathered from monitoring and assessment in New Zealand is contained in:
Carkeek, L., Davies, L., and Irwin, K. (1994). *What Happens to Māori Girls at School? An Ethnographic Study of the School-based Factors Affecting the Achievement of Māori Girls in Immersion, Bilingual, and Mainstream Primary School Programmes in the Wellington Region.*
Flockton, L. and Crooks, T. (1999). *Writing Assessment Results 1998.*
Flockton, L. and Crooks, T. (2001). *Reading and Speaking Assessment Results 2000.*
Ministry of Education (1998). *School Entry Assessment: The First National Picture – July 1997–May 1998.*
Ministry of Education (2001c). *School Entry Assessment June 1997–December 2000.*
Phillips, G., McNaughton, S., and MacDonald, S. (2000). *Picking up the Pace: Effective Literacy Interventions for Accelerated Progress over the Transition into Decile 1 Schools.*
Wylie, C. and Else, A. (1998). *Six Years Old and Competent: The Second Stage of the Competent Children Project – A Summary of the Main Findings.*

Chapter 4:
Instructional Strategies

Introduction

Instructional strategies are the tools of effective practice. They are the deliberate acts of teaching that focus learning in order to meet a particular purpose. Instructional strategies are effective only when they impact positively on students' learning.

Many studies have established that effective teachers use a range of instructional strategies. Certainly teachers need a repertoire of strategies in order to help all their students meet the challenges of becoming literate.

Instructional strategies are directed towards enabling students to build their expertise - that is, their knowledge, strategies, and awareness - in literacy learning. Skilfully used, instructional strategies generate in students the essential motivation and interest that enable them to engage in learning tasks, make connections, see how their learning is progressing, and learn how they can move on.

Being strategic as a literacy teacher involves:

- being informed by a sound knowledge of how learners acquire literacy (see chapter 2);

- selecting and using instructional strategies on the basis of a continually growing knowledge of their own students (based on sound data) and of the progressions in literacy learning (see chapter 3);

- carefully selecting texts and tasks for reading and writing in order to engage their students in rich experiences with texts (see chapter 5).

Studies consistently point to the positive impact (on students' subsequent literacy achievement) of focused instruction that begins at school entry and is sustained through the students' time at school. This is particularly true for students with limited experience of the literacy practices of schools. Teachers' knowledge of instructional strategies and their expertise in using them are crucial to achieving better outcomes for all students.

Instructional strategies are most effective when their use is planned to meet specific objectives in literacy programmes. They are also indispensable tools for teachers to use "on the run", that is, when judging what to say or do next during those unplanned interactions that continually arise during the school day.

New Zealand teachers have traditionally constructed their literacy programmes in terms of the reading and writing approaches described as "to, with, and by". These approaches are discussed on pages 90-109. Using the deliberate acts of teaching described on pages 80-87 (for example, when helping students to form intentions in their writing) will give a new focus to instruction within these approaches.

How students learn and what teachers do

The instructional strategies described on the following pages are based on well-founded understandings of what learners need to do in order to acquire literacy (and, indeed, all learning). Teachers use deliberate acts of teaching to engage learners in text-based activities.

How students learn	What teachers do
• imitate	• model • demonstrate
• identify and face challenges and overcome problems	• set instructional objectives based on students' identified needs • plan activities with appropriate kinds and levels of challenge • provide opportunities for students to solve problems
• understand and help set learning goals for tasks	• help students to understand the learning goals of tasks • build shared goals
• make connections	• show students how to activate their prior knowledge • help students to see relationships between what they know and what they are learning • monitor to ensure that students make connections
• practise	• provide opportunities for practice through text-based activities • monitor learning and plan next steps
• develop the ability to apply their learning and transfer it to new contexts	• plan opportunities for students to apply learning • show students how to use their learning in new contexts • monitor this transfer
• respond to and seek feedback	• give timely and appropriate feedback • provide opportunities for students to act on the feedback
• reflect on and regulate their learning	• help students to build metacognitive awareness • encourage students to evaluate and reflect critically on their learning

Deliberate acts of teaching

The term instructional strategy is used in this book to mean a deliberate act of teaching that focuses learning in order to meet a particular purpose.

When teachers interact with students, they use a range of deliberate acts of teaching. They use them to develop their students' knowledge, strategies, and awareness in terms of learning the code of written English, making meaning, and thinking critically when reading and writing (see pages 24–25).

The importance of deliberate, strategic teaching cannot be overemphasised. However, much learning is incidental, and improved student outcomes result from both planned and incidental learning experiences.

When using instructional strategies, teachers should be aware that they need to do the following:

- *Provide direct instruction.* Teachers cannot assume that their students will learn to read and write just through being in a literacy programme. Students need explicit, direct instruction that makes "visible" what readers and writers need to know and do.

- *Provide goal-directed instruction.* If deliberate acts of teaching are to be effective, they must be directed towards specific outcomes. Instructional strategies are the tools that teachers use to achieve their objectives (such as teaching students to monitor their learning or to use reading strategies in an integrated way).

- *Be deliberate.* Teachers need to use instructional strategies consciously and deliberately. For example, the teacher will know what they are modelling and why, or how and why they provide feedback to learners.

- *Provide a class culture and environment that facilitates learning.* The classroom conditions should facilitate learning. A print-rich physical environment is important but is not, in itself, enough. Instruction is likely to be both enjoyable and effective in a classroom that is a community of learners, where there is a climate of respect and collaboration, and where everyone sees the business of learning to read and write as something to be valued. (See chapter 8.)

- *Maintain students' motivation and enjoyment.* Students learn best when both they and their teachers find the activities enjoyable and interesting.

- *Use the same instructional strategies for teaching across the curriculum.* Teachers use their instructional strategies not only across all language and literacy activities but also in all areas of the school curriculum.

• *Be flexible and culturally responsive.* Because each learner takes an individual pathway to literacy, teachers need to be flexible in the ways they select and use instructional strategies for different activities. They should also deliberately make links between students' cultures and their classroom tasks, choosing texts and activities that incorporate familiar elements in the content, ways of communicating, and cultural practices.[27]

The effective use of instructional strategies

It is the teacher's strategic use of instruction that makes the difference. The teacher is continually making professional decisions, responding to instructional situations as a flexible problem solver, and monitoring their students' progress. Effective teachers don't follow predetermined programmes of literacy instruction. They align the literacy activities with their students' progressions.

The concept of scaffolding is useful. Scaffolding can be thought of as the purposeful use of guidance and support (through using instructional strategies) while handing over responsibility progressively to the learner. The ultimate goal is for students to self-regulate their learning and develop independence.

From the widely recognised work of Lev Vygotsky (1978) comes the notion of the zone of proximal development. Children learn most and best when they operate within their zone of proximal development – that is, when they are engaged in work that they can do with appropriate support. This zone is in between what they can do independently and what they cannot do even with support. The teacher's effective use of instructional strategies provides the help that the child needs at that point in their development.

Scaffolded instruction includes explicit explanation and modeling of a strategy, discussion of why and when it is useful, and coaching in how to apply it to novel [new] texts.
CIERA, 2002, page 1

Praise and encouragement are not listed as deliberate acts of teaching, but it is very important for teachers to praise and affirm their students in appropriate and realistic ways.

The deliberate acts of teaching described on pages 80–87 are already familiar in classrooms. They are not intended as an exhaustive list. While it's useful to distinguish among them and discuss them separately, teachers will be aware that they are used in overlapping ways and in combinations within literacy-learning activities. Pages 90–109 show deliberate acts of teaching applied in the context of the approaches to teaching reading and writing. Further practical examples appear in chapter 5.

---

[27] Refer to McNaughton (2002) and Au (2002) for evidence of the importance of making such links.

Modelling

Modelling, or "showing how", is perhaps the most powerful and pervasive form of instruction. Almost everything the teacher does and says in the course of the school day provides a potential model to the students in the classroom. Much of this modelling is implicit and occurs without either teacher or students being conscious of it. However, deliberate, goal-directed modelling is an essential teaching tool.

By articulating how they arrived at a solution – thinking aloud as they go through the process – the teacher provides a model of how a good reader or writer works. This sort of modelling makes the thinking "visible". It is a strategy used to great effect in shared reading and writing, where students are learning to use the sources of information in print along with their own prior knowledge. Modelling often involves providing the language that the learner needs.[28] This may be language for encoding or decoding text, for making meaning, or for discussing texts and thinking analytically about them.

In these examples, teachers are modelling how good readers and writers work (and are also using strategies such as questioning, prompting, and giving feedback).

"This is a new sentence. I start with a … yes, a capital letter. My first word is 'on'. What sounds can you hear? What is the first letter I write? … Let's read this sentence. Is it finished – does it make sense? Can I put in the full stop?"

"Is this how we thought Mum would feel? I'm going to read the first paragraph again. Let's list on the chart some words that might describe how Mum is feeling."

"We need some help here. We can look at the list on the wall … let's look down this list. Yes, here it tells you what to do when …"

"What word would make sense here? In the picture, we can see … Let's look at the word. It begins with a … yes, a 't'. And I can see a chunk in it …"

"That's a new word for us! We can add it to our word tree. Let's read the sentence again to see if we can find out what it means."

Sometimes modelling alone is not enough. A combination of modelling and directing (or explaining) may be necessary at times. Using modelling along with other instructional strategies to convey a teaching point is especially useful for those students who are not yet fully familiar with the literacy practices of the school and for any who are experiencing difficulties in reading or writing.

---

[28] McNaughton (2002), pages 192–193

Prompting

Prompting means encouraging the learner to use what they already know and can do. It is an effective strategy to focus students' attention and to build their metacognitive awareness and their confidence. In order to prompt effectively, the teacher needs a detailed knowledge of the learner. Prompting may take the form of a strong hint, a clue, or a gentle "nudge" to help students use their existing knowledge and literacy strategies to make connections and reach a solution. A prompt often takes the form of a question and involves allowing "wait time" to give students the opportunity to develop and express their own ideas.

These are examples of teachers using prompting strategically. Other deliberate acts of teaching can easily be identified.

Teacher	I think you could work out how to write the word "tooth".
Student	I could write down all the sounds I can hear.
Teacher	Good! Then how could you check whether you were right?

"You might need to check your conclusion again – if you look at the success criteria you may see that there's something more you need to do."

"Josh, you said 'shop', then you changed it to 'stop'. You knew something was wrong …"

"I know you know the sound for ___. Let me see you write it."

"I wonder why Dad thought Jack wasn't telling the truth. There could be a clue on this page that you just read."

"You could make those words stand out. Remember the story in guided reading yesterday. What did the words look like in the part where the farmer shouted?"

Questioning

Questioning is perhaps the instructional tool used most commonly by teachers. Strategic and purposeful questioning is crucial to students' literacy learning.

Questions may be directed towards building a particular aspect of students' knowledge, such as a strategy for encoding or decoding. At a metacognitive level, questions can help to build students' awareness. Questioning can be an ideal way to generate thoughtful discussion and help students to develop the habit of being critically reflective, for example, "How do you think …?" "I wonder why …?" "What have you noticed …?" "How will your audience feel …?" One or two well-thought-out questions can be powerful in helping students to get beyond the surface features of a text they are reading or writing. It is important that teachers ask a range of questions and know why they are asking them.

Questions become effective teaching tools when:

- they are directed towards helping students to meet a learning goal;
- they are centred on and draw out students' knowledge;
- there is adequate "wait time" for students to think through their responses;
- students' responses are valued and not transformed by evaluative comments that suggest the responses were inadequate;
- appropriate follow-up questions are used to extend students' thinking.

Such questions are a highly productive way of bringing out what students know and can do, so that they can apply their expertise to their tasks. Effective teachers extend questioning well beyond the kinds of questions that only require students to feed back factual content or to make predictions that are purely speculative.

Patterns of "teacher question, student answer, and teacher reaction" can inhibit learning. For example, if the students become more occupied with finding out what is in the teacher's head than with their own learning, they are much less likely to show creativity in composing texts or to explore deeper features of texts.

Attending to the answers that students give is as important as planning and asking the questions. Students' responses yield valuable information that can be used to evaluate their learning and to identify their next learning steps.

Teachers often categorise the kinds of questions to be used. For example, they describe questions as literal, inferential, or interpretive, as open or closed, or as questions for clarification, justification, and so on. The kinds of question and the forms they take will depend on the teacher's objective and the learning goal of the task. Sometimes closed questions will achieve the purpose, for example, when the goal is to measure students' ability to recall facts in a text, describe a process in the correct sequence, or identify a letter of the alphabet. It's not necessary or even useful to plan activities based on categories of questions. The aim is to ask questions that reveal the students' thinking, including any misconceptions or inappropriate assumptions that they may have.

Like prompting, questioning may unlock the understanding of a student who is struggling with an aspect of their reading or writing by giving them clear guidance towards what they need to do.

A teacher who uses questions effectively provides a good model to students and shows them how to develop their own questioning strategies. This helps them to bring a critical perspective to texts by asking purposeful questions of themselves as they engage with a reading or writing task. In a classroom environment of critical reflection, thought-provoking questions are not seen as threatening, they are welcomed as a highly valued part of learning.

This example shows strategic questioning to support a year 4 student in meeting the goal of a task. The context is an activity after a year 4 guided reading session using Whale Tales, *by Kim Westerskov. The shared goals are (1) to locate specific information and (2) to infer from the text and write their conclusions in their own words.*

Teacher	What information have you located?
Student	(reads) "Humpbacks swim slowly, and they are the most interesting of all whales to watch."
Teacher	OK. Do we need to take any notes there? Did you learn anything about the population or the habitat?
Student	Yeah. They have huge flippers.
Teacher	OK. So will that help us with our question?
Student	Yeah ... (uncertainly) maybe.
Teacher	(drawing student's attention to questions on whiteboard) Will that information help you to answer the question about where humpback whales live or the question on why there are only a few thousand humpbacks now?
Student	No ...
Teacher	Well, let's read the text in this box. You read it.
Student	(reading from the text) "Once, there were over 100 000 humpbacks in the southern seas alone. But the humpback was a favourite of the whalers – now there are only a few thousand humpbacks left." ... Oh. I've learned something. It says "But the humpback was a favourite of the whalers". That means that they, like, killed them, and ... that's why there aren't many living any more.
Teacher	OK. So do you think that's important information?
Student	Yes.
Teacher	Now are you going to copy that straight from the book? What are you going to do?
Student	Um, I'm going to put it in my own words.
Teacher	Good! Let me see you begin.

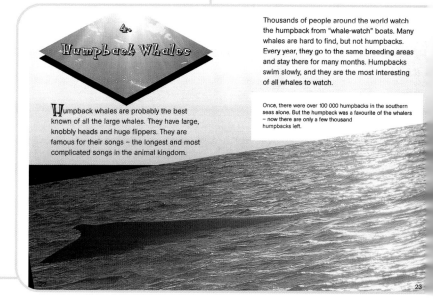

Giving feedback

The impact of effective feedback on student outcomes has been established through a number of studies (for example, Hattie, 1999, and Crooks, 1988). Hattie, on the basis of extensive research, describes feedback as the most powerful single factor that enhances achievement. Like modelling, feedback pervades the school day: most interactions between teachers and students involve some element of feedback.

The purposes of feedback are:

- to affirm;
- to inform;
- to guide future learning.

Feedback can be defined as "… providing information how and why the child understands and misunderstands, and what directions the student must take to improve" (Hattie, 1999, page 9). Like all the teaching strategies, feedback is most effective when it relates to specific learning goals and to the ultimate goal of enabling students to monitor and regulate their own learning.

Effective feedback motivates students to learn. The way that students feel about and perceive themselves affects their expectations and consequently their performance. A simple comment can have a major impact – positive or negative – on a student's motivation. It is important to consider cultural appropriateness when giving feedback (and when using any other teaching strategy).

Feedback may be thought of as either evaluative or descriptive. Evaluative feedback involves making a judgment about what the learner is doing or has done and carries the idea of approval or disapproval. Descriptive feedback means describing or explaining what has or has not been achieved and why. It also involves giving information on how to learn further or what to do next in order to succeed. Interactions involving feedback can yield valuable knowledge of learners as well as enabling them to move forward.

The primary purpose of feedback is not to indicate whether learners are right or wrong but to enable them to reflect on their use of strategies for reading and writing and on their learning. Feedback involves conveying information to learners about where and when to use their knowledge and strategies. Effective feedback can provide a model of how good readers and writers think. Feedback should be honest and specific so that learners know how they are doing. An important message for teachers to convey to students is that using effective strategies in their reading and writing is what caused their success; this is crucial to building students' metacognition. It's especially useful to encourage students themselves to suggest what they could do. This is a great way to build their awareness of how they can take control of their learning.

Feedback may be verbal or non-verbal, spoken or written. The quality of the teacher's written feedback on a student's writing is especially important, both for providing further guidance and for the student's confidence.

The teacher should not allow their feedback to take over the ownership of the learning task. For example, a teacher may be tempted to "improve" a student's piece of writing, with the result that the student's voice or sense of ownership may be lost (even though the teacher may feel that the work is better crafted).

Success criteria that arise from shared goals give valuable focus to teachers' conversations with students and to the feedback that they provide. It is essential to ensure that the students understand the information conveyed through feedback and to provide time and opportunity for them to act on it.

> *These examples show effective use of feedback in several literacy contexts. In giving such feedback, teachers are also providing good models to the students.*
>
> "Well done. You have seen that from another point of view. What reasons can you give to back up your opinion?"
>
> "I like the way you've started your sentences in different ways – it makes it more interesting for the reader. I can imagine what your grandma is like by reading your story."
>
> "That was good thinking. I could see you used the pictures and the title to help you make that prediction."
>
> "I noticed that you went to our reference texts to help you find the information. That's good use of research skills. Next time, you could try the websites listed for our topic study."
>
> "You looked at the end of the word carefully – you fixed it yourself."
>
> | | |
> |---|---|
> | Teacher | What else could you tell us about the big storm? You've told us where you were and how you felt. |
> | Jane | I could say how it sounded. |
> | Teacher | That's a great idea – storms are always noisy. What words can you think of? |
> | Jane | Roaring ... howling ...? |
> | Teacher | Oh, I can hear it! You need to think about where to put this new information in. |

Telling

At its simplest level, telling means supplying what the student needs, such as an unknown word or a topic for a literacy-learning task. The idea is to fill a gap at that moment to enable the student to move on.

A strategic use of telling may involve providing the language needed to participate in an activity. The teacher tells the students how to spell the word they need for a piece of writing or, at the beginning of a reading task, tells them the theme of the text. This may be the most effective way to work with some students who do not have the background knowledge on which to base productive prediction. Simply providing a label or definition may be the most efficient way to move a student's learning on.

Telling can also mean providing information about when to use a particular literacy strategy in a given task – making explicit the fact that the students can apply their existing knowledge at this point and so building their awareness of when to apply that knowledge in future situations. Telling students when to apply their expertise is particularly useful for students who are experiencing difficulties in reading or writing.

Examples of a teacher making a strategic decision to supply what the students need at that moment may be:

"Today we're going to focus on ..."

"That word is_____. It means_____. Now read on."

"This book that we are going to read tells us about all the ..."

"When you write 'stopping', you need two p's."

"This is a new idea. You need to start a new paragraph."

Explaining

Explaining can be thought of as an extension of telling. Teachers may explain the task itself, or they may explain the content of a text or learning activity. For example, the teacher may explain:

- what they want the students to do while reading a particular text;
- how a certain task will help the students to achieve a particular goal;
- how procedural text is set out;
- the background to a topic (for example, as an introduction to a writing activity).

Teachers also use explanations in the context of classroom management (for example, when they explain what is involved in an activity such as paired reading) so that all the students can participate confidently.

The following examples show explanation in relation to text content and a text feature.

In a shared reading session, the teacher and children read together until the word "thistles", which the teacher reads.

Ethan	What are thistles?
Sally	Flowers?
Teacher	Thistles are like prickles. They have a pretty flower on the top, but if you touch thistles, they feel like prickles. They are a problem for farmers. But goats are great on farms because goats will eat anything. Even prickles.

"Look at the text in the blue box. It tells you what equipment the men needed to help move the building. This information is not part of the main story, so it is shown in a different way so that the reader can see that it's something separate."

A characteristic of explanations is that they are verbally explicit. Careful explanations enable students to develop their own understandings. Throughout the many interactions that occur during the school day, the teacher needs to be alert and ready to explain things, picking up cues from the students and adapting their use of this teaching strategy to supply what each learner needs. Sometimes a direct approach is best ("Let me explain this to you"), especially for students who are not yet familiar with the established classroom literacy activities.

Directing

Directing is simply giving a specific instruction. Like all these instructional strategies, it is used deliberately, for a purpose.

Everyday classroom examples of directing are:

"Put your finger on ..."

"Write the letter for that sound."

"Find the part in your piece of writing that ..."

"Turn to your buddy and discuss why ..."

"Look at the checklist on the wall if you're stuck."

Integrating instructional strategies

This final example shows several of these strategies being used in combination in a typical interaction during shared reading. The teacher is modelling, giving feedback, questioning, and prompting.

Teacher	Let's see who he watched on Monday.[29] Who is he watching?
Ethan	(looking at illustration) He's watching the cat.
Teacher	What's the cat's work?
Ethan	(again drawing from illustration) Chasing the mice.
Teacher	Let's read it together and see if you're right. (reads) "On Monday he w... (pauses) watched the cat. She ..." Oh. How does the cat move?
Several children	She p... r... [they make separate sounds]
Oliver	pr...
Children	... prowls!
Teacher	Good boy for getting that blend, Oliver. (reads slowly, drawing out the new word, and the children join in) "She pr–owled up and down looking for mice."

A number of the interactions and examples appearing throughout this book also show these deliberate acts of teaching in use in a range of contexts.

---

[29] The text used is *Lazy Duck* by J. Windsor.

Classroom conversations

Classroom conversations provide a vehicle for involving students as joint constructors of their learning. Purposeful conversation or discussion has a wide range of uses.

Classroom conversations should be directed towards a goal. The teacher knows why the discussion is being held and what the desired outcome is. Purposeful discussion provides an obvious context for the strategic use of feedback, modelling, questions, explanations, and so on. It is valuable for building students' metacognitive awareness; for example, a teacher may discuss, with a student or group, the strategies that the student(s) used to compose in their writing or to solve a problem in their reading.

For quality conversations, mutual trust is a prerequisite. The teacher listens and responds with empathy, openly valuing all students' experience and expertise. Relationships and interactions in classroom conversations tend to reflect power balances, and so teachers may need to address this issue. Studies have shown that teachers' expectations of and assumptions about certain groups of students can influence the patterns of student participation in conversations.[30]

In effective classroom conversations, the teacher is not content with minimal responses and constantly leads the students to extend the depth and breadth of their knowledge and language use. The students are fully engaged and participate actively.

Teachers have a crucial role in:

- enabling students to "own" their statements, opinions, and responses;
- supporting students in actively talking about how they make meaning and develop awareness in their written-language activities;
- clarifying their own understanding of what each student says;
- creating an environment where students can converse without feeling that they have to wait for the teacher's evaluative comment on what they say.

A classroom conversation can be a simple interchange between a student and the teacher to clarify an understanding. The teacher may plan an interview with a student, for example, a conference on their writing. Some classroom conversations are discussions between students interacting in groups or in pairs (such as reading buddies). Focused talk about a text, in shared reading or writing sessions, is a great way to build students' vocabulary as well as their knowledge of text forms and features. Conversations between the teacher and a group of students are an essential element in guided reading sessions, where focused discussion of the text draws out the students' understandings and fosters critical thinking.

---

[30] Refer, for example, to Glynn, Berryman, and Glynn (2000).

Teachers' choice and use of language in classroom conversation is very important. They should be clear and precise, especially in giving instructions and feedback. Consistency and clarity in the teacher's talk provide a good model for learners and show them how to communicate successfully.

Students from backgrounds where children are not encouraged to question what an adult says, or where they are expected to be receptive rather than active learners, may be guided sensitively towards feeling comfortable about responding or expressing their point of view. It is important for them to learn these kinds of practices in order to succeed at school and later on.

Focused conversations can support students in becoming interpretive readers and writers so that they develop the habit of being thoughtful and critically aware when reading or composing text. Many theoretical studies have focused on critical thinking in literacy learning. Marie Clay has gathered up these thoughts, describing her observation of teachers in their interactions with children:

> *The teachers restated what children told them, they modeled new things children could do, they helped children try new things, they linked what the child was aware of to some other experiences known to the child, they shaped the child's product a little toward the desired goal, and they did some of the work for the child if that achieved the child's goal (for example, writing a new letter or a difficult word into the child's story). Often the teacher invited the child to elaborate on what he or she had already said – verbal elaboration that I called "talk more."...*

> *... if we use something like the conversation model in our teaching and think about how to link into the listener's knowledge every time we hold a conversation, we might be more helpful to children, and from our model they might learn how to make connections for themselves. Encouraging young children to talk more about their understandings is one way of helping them to make connections.*

Clay, 1998, page 32

Approaches to reading and writing

Teachers employ the deliberate acts of teaching discussed above to help their students reach a number of essential literacy-related goals. These include:

- developing word analysis skills;
- learning comprehension strategies;
- learning composition strategies;
- building vocabulary;
- developing higher level thinking skills in order to go more deeply into the texts that they read and write;
- learning to use different language structures for different purposes.

Such objectives are achieved in New Zealand classrooms through a variety of text-based activities within a range of approaches and other contexts that have proved highly effective. The range includes language experience activities, reading to children, shared reading and writing, guided reading and writing, independent reading and writing, literature circles, reciprocal teaching, and mini-lessons.

Mini-lessons

This term describes a short period of explicit instruction (in a specific skill or item of knowledge) that arises from a need the teacher has identified for a student or group. The teacher will take the instruction on into subsequent text-based activities.

Sometimes a mini-lesson is planned in advance because it fits in with the planned objective of, for example, a guided reading session. At other times, it is simply a matter of seizing the "teachable moment". An immediate learning need becomes apparent during an activity, and the teacher makes a judgment about whether to give the focused instruction right then or to take it up afterwards. Either way, the principle is that a need has arisen and that the teacher acts deliberately and purposefully to address it.

We put our new clothes in the car,
but when we tried to put
the table in, it didn't fit.
We had to carry it all the way home!
Then we had to walk back
to get the car.

10

The teacher has kept back two children after a guided reading session.

Teacher   Today, when you were reading *The Garage Sale*,[31] you didn't seem to notice the commas, and I saw you getting into a bit of a muddle on page 10. I want you to read that first sentence on page 10 again, and each time you come to a comma, I want you to pause. Try it now.

(The children read, pausing at the commas.)

Teacher   That's right – when they "tried to put the table in, it didn't fit." Remember that commas are there to help you make sense of what you read. They show which words belong together, so you need to notice them when you're reading. I'll be listening for how you notice the commas tomorrow!

[31] *The Garage Sale* by F. Hunia

Approaches to reading

Reading to children

Reading aloud from the best of children's literature should be a daily part of every classroom programme at all levels. Listening to a story told or read aloud well is a captivating experience.

Reading aloud to children frees them from the labour of decoding and supports them in becoming active listeners, totally engaged and immersed in the text. As children create meaning from a text by making connections between what they already know and what they hear, they develop new knowledge and awareness. They enrich their vocabulary by hearing new words in context and familiar words used in new ways, and they develop new insights into the way language works (for example, how words can be ordered and how imagery can be used) and into the different text forms. A great deal of implicit learning occurs when children are read to.

Reading aloud is appropriate for all students, including those who already read accurately and fluently. This teaching approach can be used effectively with both large and small groups. Students who have had limited experiences with books, or who are receptive rather than active learners, can benefit when they are read to in small groups and the teacher can encourage them to engage with the text and respond to it actively.

We'd been studying tales and myths of Aotearoa and Pasifika countries. I chose *Māui and the Sun*[32] for this group because I thought they would like a superhero who overcomes the forces of nature. The elements of the traditional tale are all here – the cunning plot, the brothers-in-arms, the struggle. It's short but full of action, so I was able to read it twice in one session. The style of illustration sets the Māori context well, and when we looked at the detail after they had heard the story, the children were intrigued by the changing expressions on the face of the sun. The strong narrative has suspense and action, and it kept the children engaged. I dramatised the reading by heightening the different voices of the characters – Māui, the brothers, and the sun. I emphasised the repetition of some phrases – "and plenty of ...", for instance – and when I read it again, Aaron and Tu both chimed in on the second "Let me go!" I'll follow this up with another Māui story soon.

Teacher, year 2 class

[32] *Māui and the Sun* by J. Melser

Māui and the Sun

retold by June Melser
pictures by Cliff Whiting

When reading to children, the teacher acts on behalf of the author, presenting the writing with as much enthusiasm and commitment as if it were his or her own. The teacher is the vehicle for the book's voice ...

Mooney, 1988, page 24

Reading to children is an approach that can be used strategically in order to:

- promote and foster a love of reading;
- develop vocabulary and a knowledge of book language and text forms;
- develop awareness of the sounds, rhythms, and patterns of language;
- engage children in conversations about texts;
- encourage children to respond imaginatively to a variety of texts;
- promote oral language development;
- develop skills in listening comprehension and critical thinking;
- provide opportunities for children to visualise aspects of a text;
- help children to develop effective strategies for dealing with unfamiliar vocabulary and building meaning;
- support children who are learning English;
- create opportunities for retelling and ideas for writing.

Choosing texts

When selecting texts for reading to children, teachers are guided by their own instructional objectives and by the students' interests and cultural values. Refer to page 114 in chapter 5 for discussion about the importance of using a range and variety of texts.

Reading the text

The way the teacher reads aloud is very important. Teachers may need to practise so that they know the story well and can relax and concentrate on reading expressively. Such reading provides a good model for students and conveys many implicit messages about literacy learning. Above all, it demonstrates in the best possible way that reading is important and that books are a source of delight.

Supporting students' responses

Depending on their teaching objectives, the nature of the text, and the students' interest, the teacher may encourage the students' responses and their predictions or conversations about the text (without interrupting the flow of the text and the listeners' enjoyment). Effective teachers enable their students to savour the experience, share their enthusiasm, and reflect on new words, expressions, or ideas.

I read to the class every day, and it's a special time for us. The emphasis is on enjoyment, but I've become more focused in selecting texts. Recently I read *The Three Little Wolves and the Big Bad Pig*,[33] a nice reversal of the traditional tale. We'd been looking at the great themes of conflict and resolution in traditional literature. I also wanted to develop the students' listening comprehension. In addition, about one-third of my class are NESB students who need to encounter many literary texts in English.

We all enjoyed the fun of the story, and all tuned in and became engaged with the narrative. Then we got into a debate about what made the big bad pig become friends with the little wolves and whether this was a good thing to happen. What I'm finding is that rich conversations around texts show what thinkers these students really are – and it's got nothing to do with whether they are the more able readers in the class or not. It's a matter of giving the students the opportunity to process ideas and share their views. I also notice increasing participation by those from diverse cultural backgrounds, who may not be used to expressing a point of view.

Teacher, years 3 to 4

Shared reading

Shared reading is an essential component of the daily literacy programme. It allows for a high degree of interaction and is a great way for teachers to help students to increase their understanding of themselves as text users. It's an effective approach, which can be used with both large groups and small groups to develop students' strategies and their knowledge of how written texts work (see page 27).

When a teacher reads to students, the students participate as active listeners. In shared reading, the teacher and the students read a text together. The teacher leads the reading, and the students follow with their eyes, actively listening, and join in as they become familiar with words, phrases, or concepts. All the participants need to be able to see the text, which is usually enlarged. The teacher's support enables the students to behave like readers and enjoy the text even though they may not yet be able to read it comfortably on their own.

Shared reading conveys messages about the joys of reading. It also provides a supportive instructional setting in which teachers can systematically and purposefully:

- develop positive attitudes towards reading;
- model fluent, expressive reading;
- deliberately teach specific strategies for reading;
- develop students' awareness of visual and phonological information;
- teach specific vocabulary and identify particular word features;
- build students' understanding of text forms and structures;

---

[33] *The Three Little Wolves and the Big Bad Pig* by E. Trivizas

- encourage thoughtful and personal responses, including critical responses, to text;
- develop a sense of community in the classroom;
- expose students to a wide range of texts.

The same text can be used several times in successive shared reading sessions, with a different focus each time to meet new goals. As the students become familiar with the text, they gradually take more responsibility for reading it themselves.

Students for whom English is a new language can participate confidently in shared reading. They attend to the illustrations, diagrams, and photographs while hearing the language used in an enjoyable and authentic context.

Shared reading provides opportunities for teachers to observe how their students interact with texts. It also allows teachers to plan purposeful ways to develop students' use of the sources of information in text (see pages 28-31) in a supportive context. It's an ideal setting in which to introduce and reinforce information about the conventions of print (see page 33), about strategies for solving unknown words, and about sound patterns in spoken language (see pages 32-37) or spelling patterns in written language (see pages 144-148). Refer also to the sections on shared reading in the Ministry of Education's *Ready to Read Teacher Support Material)*.

Choosing texts

A wide range of different types of text should be selected for shared reading. Each text should be chosen to suit one or more specific instructional purposes. From the beginning years, the range should include non-fiction. Shared reading can also incorporate handmade texts, poems, songs, pieces from magazines, and articles from newspapers – perhaps enlarged for use on the overhead projector. An overhead projector can also be used to display the menus, web pages, and icons that enable readers to navigate electronic texts on the Internet.

Shared reading sessions

A shared reading session may last as long as twenty minutes, depending on the purposes, the time of day, and the students' interest. Alternatively, it may be a brief session, simply to savour a favourite text or to reread something that captures the moment.

Introducing the text

A text should be introduced in a way that builds eagerness and a sense of anticipation. Keeping the introduction brief helps the students to relate the text to their experience and to predict something of its meaning and structure. The purpose for reading the text should be shared with the students.

Reading the text

The first reading should focus on the students' enjoyment and understanding of the text. With texts that have a catchy rhythm and repetitive pattern, the students can

be encouraged to join in on the first reading. Teachers often engage learners by pausing and asking them to predict what may happen next or to share their responses briefly.

In subsequent readings, the teacher can focus on specific features or learning strategies that they have identified for teaching or reinforcement with the group. This could involve writing words on the whiteboard to explore spelling patterns or letter-sound relationships. (A masking device may be used to isolate letters, words, or parts of words.) Or the focus could be on features of layout, such as bold headings, and on helping the students to find out how to use these features in their reading and their writing. Another focus could be on close reading of a particular passage to help the students identify the main points or the words that indicate a particular character's point of view.

All the children loved *Clickety-Clack Cicada*.[34] They recognised the insect as soon as I put the poem card on the easel, and they shuddered and giggled about the way cicadas cling to you. The alliteration and rhythm helped my two newly arrived children to join in the reading.

I used the mask to reinforce the contraction of "don't", to teach the letter blend "cl", and to demonstrate the different sounds of "c" within the word "cicada". The children thought of other examples of the blend "cl", including "class", "clean", "clap", and "clever". I'll draw the children's attention to the spelling of "circle" and "centre" when we're doing maths and look for opportunities in guided and shared reading to draw children's attention to the different sounds of "c".

We also focused on the difference, in the poem, between the quiet night and the noisy day. We'll read and talk about other insect and animal poems, and we'll build up a collection of words and phrases for the children to use in their own writing.

Teacher, year 1 class

[34] *Clickety-Clack Cicada* by J. Brasell

Following up

Shared reading texts should be made available after the reading so that the students can enjoy them independently. Small groups can use enlarged texts and charts (or audio versions if these are available) to replicate the shared reading experience. The students can take turns to lead the group in reading, using a pointer.

Some texts lend themselves to further activities, depending on the teacher's objectives. Activities might include:

- shared writing modelled on the text;
- word-level work, such as listing words that have the same rime;
- retelling the story to a small group;
- dramatising episodes of the story;
- improvising music to accompany a dramatisation of the story.

Simply hearing the text again, possibly at a listening post, may be the most appropriate follow-up.

Guided reading

In any literacy programme, guided reading has a central role in leading students towards independence in reading.[35] The focused group setting enables the teacher to provide strategic instruction in decoding, making meaning, and thinking critically.

During guided reading, the teacher works with a small group of students who have similar instructional needs so that they are supported in reading a text successfully by themselves. Each student has a copy of the text. It should contain some challenges, which should be at a level that the students can manage as they individually read the text in the supportive situation.

Guided reading provides a framework in which teachers can use instructional strategies to:

- help students to develop an understanding of what is involved in reading and an expectation of success;
- help students to learn, practise, and integrate their reading strategies;
- help students to read new text successfully;
- monitor students closely while they engage with and process texts;
- develop students' comprehension of and critical responses to text;
- build students' confidence as independent readers;
- show students how the processes of reading and writing are integral to each other.

Students gain most from guided reading when they have developed a number of understandings about text. These are usually best gained through shared reading and oral language activities. Observation and monitoring of what the student knows

---

[35] *Guided Reading* is a resource comprising a book and two videos showing guided reading in some detail. See also the sections on guided reading in the Ministry of Education's *Ready to Read Teacher Support Material.*

and can do will guide the teacher's decision about when to begin the more intensive guided reading approach.

Forming groups for guided reading demands thought and judgment. Each group should be small enough for intensive support, but there should not be so many groups that class management becomes unwieldy. Since students progress at different rates, guided reading groups will change as the students' competencies change.

Before the session

Deciding on the focus or purpose of the session
Both the teacher and the students need to be clear about the purpose for reading the text. The focus for instruction could be, for example, on:

- using word-level information to decode new words;
- using illustrations to support or extend understanding of a text;
- looking at character development in a story;
- predicting the outcome of a story;
- using a table of contents, chart, or table;
- interpreting quotation or question marks;
- introducing a new text form;
- inferring from actions or dialogue.

Selecting an appropriate text
Given the central role of texts in literacy development, text selection is a crucial step. Teachers base their selection on their instructional objectives and on their knowledge of the learners, ensuring that the texts are appropriate to the students' learning needs and relate to their interests and experiences. Generally, the text will be new to the students, although beginning readers may have met it before in shared reading. (Sometimes, though, it is appropriate to select familiar material in order to focus on a specific language or literary feature.) As a general rule, texts for guided reading should be at a level where students have no more than five to ten difficulties in every hundred words. See chapter 5 for discussion of text features and of the supports and challenges in texts.

Planning for the session
Planning for the session involves:

- deciding how to introduce the text;
- identifying challenges that the text might present and deciding how to address them;
- considering how to generate discussion to take the students further into the text;
- deciding on related follow-up activities if appropriate.

During the session

Introducing the text

The introduction to the session should be brief and build a sense of expectancy. It should share the purpose for the reading and focus on relating the text to the students' experiences and interests. The teacher may discuss or explain particular features or potential challenges that the students may need help with, such as names of characters, captions for diagrams, or technical terms.

The teacher then sets the reading task by directing the group to read the text or a section of it and telling them what they are to think about or find out.

Reading the text

The students take responsibility for reading the text themselves individually. With longer texts, where more complex challenges may arise, the reading can be "chunked" into two or more sections, with a brief discussion between sections to sustain comprehension. As they become more fluent, the students may be encouraged to read silently.

During the reading, as they monitor each member of the group, the teacher can encourage the students by prompting them to use the strategies that they have learned. The teacher may move alongside a student to check how they are processing the text. But, during the reading, the teacher should intervene only when necessary. A short, purposeful task for those who are likely to finish earlier than others is useful.

Discussing the text

Generating purposeful, stimulating discussion around a text is perhaps the greatest challenge in guided reading. Focused discussion is central to this approach, because a fundamental purpose of guided reading is to enhance each student's understanding of what they are reading. The focus and length of the discussion will reflect the shared goal for the session, the level of the students' interest and engagement, and the demands of the text.

The teacher's role is to:

- maintain the focus by skilled use of questioning, prompting, or modelling of what good readers do;
- encourage the students' personal responses and sharing of insights;
- encourage genuine conversations in which responses and points of view are valued;
- help the students to explore text features and challenges;
- encourage the students to share how they worked out unknown words or drew inferences from the text;
- develop the students' comprehension and critical thinking;
- probe the students' understandings and ask them to clarify their statements where necessary;

> "Round robin" reading, where each student takes a turn at reading aloud, is never appropriate in guided reading. It prevents each student from processing the text and constructing meaning independently, distracts and bores other children, and obscures meaning.

- ask the students to justify a statement or opinion by going back to the text;
- model ways of responding critically to text (for example, by using questions or thought-provoking comments);
- foster enjoyment of the text and a sense of discovery;
- give feedback that is specific, that informs, and that builds further understanding.

For beginning readers, the focus is on getting through the reading successfully. As students become more fluent, more time will be spent in discussion and comparatively less in reading. But, from the beginning, students should expect to think and talk about what they are reading. The discussion should be enjoyable and engaging for both students and teachers.

Using an easel or whiteboard gives a visual focus, for example, when:

- examining word-level features, such as letter-sound relationships, spelling patterns, onsets and rimes, and new vocabulary;
- recording and plotting the main ideas or facts in the text;
- noting words or ideas that sparked debate, to return to later.

See also the section about classroom conversations on pages 88–89 and refer to *Guided Reading: Years 1–4*, pages 45–49.

Concluding the session

At the end of a guided reading session, it's important to review, with the group, the original purpose of the session and to ensure that it has been met. It's also valuable to encourage the students to reflect on their learning and talk about it so that they develop awareness of how to use and control what they know and can do. This will enable them to increasingly monitor their own progress.

I had read *A Quilt for Kiri* [36] to the children last term, and I retold the story last week. As a class, we had talked then about customs of giving gifts – what we give people and when – and the idea that gifts we've made ourselves have extra value. Three of the children are from the Cook Islands and were able to tell us more about quilts, so we talked about that and other traditions for showing appreciation for kindness or hospitality. I chose *A Gift for Aunty Ngā* [37] for guided reading with my fluent readers. I wanted to focus on critical thinking and inference, and they found a great deal to consider in this moving story about family relationships and separations. I asked them to read just the first two pages, and then we talked about what they could infer. They anticipated the forthcoming trip and also realised that the "tapes" showed that the family rarely saw Aunty Ngā. They then read on to the end of page 7, and we talked again about the trip and what they thought about the relationship between Kiri and her aunt. When they had finished their reading, there was rich discussion about the characters, the children's own experiences, the meaning of gifts, and the way we celebrate big occasions. All the children wanted to reread the text to savour it for themselves.

Teacher, year 3 class

---

[36] *A Quilt for Kiri* by D. Long

[37] *A Gift for Aunty Ngā* by D. Long

After the session

Most teachers make the book available for the students to reread to a buddy or by themselves. Often, children also take the book home to share with their family. These repeated readings give the students opportunities to enjoy the text personally, practise newly acquired strategies, absorb new information, and develop fluency.

It is valuable to jot down observations on individual students' progress and to note teaching points for the future.

The text may lend itself to further activities. These may be planned beforehand to help meet the teacher's objectives, but others may arise as result of monitoring during the session. Such activities may include:

- making a timeline, story map, chart, or graph;
- writing character sketches;
- sorting or generating word lists, such as "words beginning with a prefix" (for example, "un-");
- retelling the text or innovating on the text;
- creating art work and adding captions;
- reading other texts with a similar theme or form;
- a mini-lesson to teach or reinforce a reading strategy.

However, often the reading is sufficient in itself, and the best follow-up activity is simply lots more reading.[38]

Independent reading

Reading at home and at school should be relaxed and enjoyable. Parents and teachers demonstrate that they value reading when they read themselves and also make sure that students have time to enjoy reading.

For students, independent reading of material they choose themselves:

- builds the habit of reading;
- allows them to practise reading strategies with books that interest them;
- builds their vocabulary and helps comprehension;
- helps them to sustain concentrated reading for a set time;
- promotes fluency;
- puts the responsibility for solving problems with words and meaning into their own hands;
- helps to build their confidence about trying unfamiliar books.

Studies have documented evidence linking children's access to books, and the amount of reading that they do, to their achievement in reading. Choosing to read recreationally is also associated with high rates of achievement.

---

[38] For examples of ways of using Ready to Read texts for guided reading, refer to the notes for individual titles in the Ministry of Education's *Ready to Read Teacher Support Material.*

A set time in the daily routine for independent reading by individual students is an essential part of the classroom literacy programme. If they are to become lifelong readers, students need to choose to read, select their own texts, and share what they have read. Ready access to a wide range of interesting materials that they can read by themselves is also important because it enables the students to choose to read independently whenever an opportunity arises. Teachers need to make it clear that students benefit greatly when they engage in recreational reading, both in and out of school.

The teacher needs to establish routines and expectations so that all students move naturally from reading aloud to silent reading. Silent, independent reading has proven benefits and is associated with student achievement. As their students gain fluency and independence, teachers should plan to model and teach silent and attentive reading. Students also achieve better when they see their teacher reading independently for pleasure.[39]

During independent reading, teachers should observe the students' reading behaviour and monitor their interest and enthusiasm, their selection of texts, their understanding of what they read, and the amount of reading they do. This will inform the teacher's future guidance of each student's reading.

Informal, focused individual or small-group conferences can yield valuable information about what the students are reading, whether they are setting themselves new challenges, and how they are enjoying the books they choose. The teacher may use a student's reading log, for example, when prompting and questioning, to draw the student's attention to their patterns of reading and to ways of extending these patterns. However, it's important at all times to avoid being intrusive – independent reading is intensely personal and should focus on enjoyment.

The connection between the amount of reading done and reading proficiency has been well known and accepted for a number of years. Less well known but of equal importance has been the finding that more access to reading materials leads to more reading, and subsequently higher reading achievement … access to books in school via the library was the most powerful predictor of academic achievement among several variables analyzed, controlling for socioeconomic status.
McQuillan, 1998, pages 72–73

Reciprocal teaching

Reciprocal teaching is a useful small-group procedure to help improve the comprehension and critical thinking of fluent readers. Studies have shown that when students take part in reciprocal teaching of reading, their comprehension improves (including their listening comprehension) and they transfer the learning into other reading contexts.[40] Reciprocal teaching has been found to be effective in improving the achievement of learners from diverse backgrounds. It involves four explicit strategies for reading comprehension:

- formulating questions to stimulate thoughtful discussion;
- clarifying ideas in the text;
- predicting what might follow, using prior knowledge and information in the text;
- summarising information in the text.

The teacher initially leads the group, explaining and modelling the strategies to show how the reader actively constructs meaning. The students gradually take over more

Reciprocal teaching and literature circles are not usually thought of as approaches to reading but provide useful contexts for developing literacy learning.

---

[39] Refer to the studies reported in Smith and Elley (1997a), pages 41–43.

[40] For example, refer to Smith and Elley (1997a), pages 55–56, and McNaughton (2002), pages 154–159.

and more of the responsibility by taking turns to lead the group and generate discussion as the group members jointly examine and interpret a text.[41]

Literature circles

Many teachers use literature circles as a way of encouraging their students to think and talk about a wide range of texts. As students develop their skills in reading and in expressing ideas, they can join in these groups. In a literature circle, the students generate the discussion, which is based on their own interpretations of the text. Small groups of students read the same book independently and share their personal responses and interpretations with others in the group. Having the students mark parts of the book helps to focus their discussion of a text, for example, where they:

- find a passage confusing;
- want to ask the group questions about the plot, characters, or information;
- can relate an event in the book to personal experience;
- find the language beautiful or memorable;
- find a part of the story very exciting, entertaining, or moving;
- want to talk about a diagram or a dramatic photograph.

Approaches to writing

Language experience activities

Language experience activities are a way of motivating learners that can lead into meaningful writing (including shared or guided writing). Language experience activities involve planned, purposeful "doing and talking" together, which will be followed by writing and reading about the experience. Such activities help young learners to make sense of their world by taking part in, sharing, and discussing authentic experiences and (usually) going on to contribute to or construct a written text about them.

The teacher engages the students in the experience and in discussion that elicits the students' own language about the experience, some of which is generally recorded on a whiteboard. The teacher may go on to use shared or guided writing to produce the text or texts about the experience. The key feature of this approach is that it uses talk about children's experiences as the basis for writing.

A great deal of implicit learning occurs during language experience activities. Many messages are conveyed about the nature of writing, how print works, and the conventions of various forms of written language.

Language experience activities make visible the links between spoken and written language. A lot of talk takes place, and the children become aware that writing arises from oral language. As the children enjoy reading and rereading the texts that they have created, they build their awareness of the relationship between reading and writing.

---

[41] For further information about reciprocal teaching, refer to pages 55–56 of Smith and Elley (1997a) or to the Ministry of Education's video resource *Reciprocal Teaching: Extending Reading Strategies* (1993), which shows the procedure being used at middle to senior primary levels.

Language experience activities also provide opportunities for teachers to meet instructional objectives in particular subject areas and to develop literacy learning across the curriculum.

This example describes a series of language experience activities in a small rural school. The school also used the "eels" topic for wider cross-curriculum work (see pages 173–176).

One focus of the experience was catching eels and keeping them in a glass tank in the classroom. The children were able to observe the eels in the tank and to feed them. This generated huge enthusiasm. Children who were generally reluctant to share (especially some of the boys) suddenly had lots to say about their own eeling trips.

Together, we brainstormed words to describe what eels look like, how they move, and what they feel like. We added new words to a whiteboard as the children thought of them. The children relished adding and repeating words like "flappy", "gooey", "slimy", "slippery", "creepy", "sloppy", and "slithery". I used the opportunity to draw attention to the "ee" sound of "y".

We used the experience to meet many objectives. We read informational and literary texts in shared and guided reading and researched to find further information. The children drew and labelled diagrams and wrote poems. Collaboratively, we wrote a big book modelled on Patricia Grace's *Watercress Tuna and the Children of Champion Street*. The children discovered technical and scientific terms. They still talk about "migration", "metamorphosis", and "hypotheses" – terms that my five- and six-year-olds met for the first time through this experience.

The children, most of whom are Māori, felt a high level of ownership of the learning – it had personal value for them. The experience and related activities affirmed their cultural values around something that was of traditional significance in their community.

What I want my children to understand is that what they experience can not only be talked about; it can also be written down, and in *their* words. The big book we made at the time, capturing their own words, is still in constant use months later.

Language experience involves providing children with experiences that encourage them to explore, think, and feel. Such experiences enrich children's speaking and listening and lead on naturally to their writing and reading. …
Ready to Read Teacher Support Material: Early Levels, page 10

Teachers plan interesting, enjoyable language experiences with an instructional purpose in mind. These experiences help children to think about what they would like to write. For example, the teacher may use:

- special events within the school, such as a fair, a sports day, or a visit;
- special events beyond the school, such as a celebration or another local or national occasion;
- a practical activity, such as cooking or painting.

Language experience activities allow the teacher and children to develop a shared language as together they use the language orally and discuss how to transform it into writing. The teacher models writing down some of the key words and phrases that arise in the discussion.

During discussion, meanings are clarified, and so the conversation can be extended. The students' ideas are explored, and their words are recorded, by the teacher in shared writing or by the student in guided writing.

Such writing is deeply personal because it reflects the children's voices directly. The teacher has a strategic role in ensuring that each child has ownership of what is written. One reason why language experience activities are so effective with new learners of English and students from diverse cultural backgrounds is that the experience can capture and affirm what is of personal value to each student.

Learner writers may express their ideas first in drawing. Teachers can gain a lot of information from their students' drawings, for example, by observing the subject matter they choose and the details they include.

Shared writing

Shared writing involves the teacher and a group of students – often the whole class – in planning and constructing a text together. The teacher models and talks through the process of constructing a text (or part of one), giving explicit instruction in how to use writing strategies during the shared writing process. The students contribute their ideas and expertise to the process of constructing the text. (This is often followed by guided writing; when the teacher has constructed part of a text, the students continue writing their own texts, working with teacher support but as individual writers.) Through shared writing, students can take part in constructing a more complex text than they would be able to write on their own.

Modelling can be used as an instructional strategy to show students, step by step, the planning, shaping, and structuring of a text for a specific purpose. The teacher may model the use of a "mind map" or "web" to show how a writer assembles ideas and then sorts them to be ready for writing. Carefully planned questions can help the students to think about how a particular text might be organised. The teacher may prompt by showing them similar familiar material or by reviewing with them the features of a particular type of text.

This approach enables the teacher to expose students to new, rich language, adding to the range of vocabulary and language structures that they can use in their personal writing. Shared writing reinforces positive attitudes towards writing by making it an enjoyable and creative activity.

The shared writing approach is not just for beginners. In years 3 and 4 and beyond, teachers can help their students to develop more complex ideas and language and can foster their critical awareness as writers. Shared writing provides an excellent context for introducing or reinforcing information about the features of texts, including the features of the kinds of non-fiction texts that students will later encounter in science, mathematics, and other curriculum areas.

The teacher begins by sharing the purpose for the shared writing session with the students. During the session, the teacher acts as scribe, writing on a chart or whiteboard in front of the students and showing them how to construct a coherent and enjoyable text. Over a series of shared writing sessions, the whole process of writing a text may be modelled – forming intentions, composing, revising, and publishing for an audience (see pages 138–141). Generally, however, the product of shared writing is intended to meet an immediate purpose, so the group will focus on only one part of the process.

Topics for shared writing can arise from many sources, including:

- current events and situations in the students' lives;
- current themes in cross-curricular work;
- readings that the students have shared;
- artefacts or objects that the students have handled and discussed;
- discoveries in the natural environment;
- hobbies or school activities that the students take part in;
- images from wordless picture books, photo sequences, or paintings.

Shared writing provides a supportive instructional setting in which (depending on their students' learning needs) teachers can:

- model the process of writing;
- explain and model the use of the conventions of written text;
- explicitly teach writing strategies;
- analyse how words are constructed;
- focus on letters, words, and letter-sound relationships;
- explore letter clusters, words within words, and patterns of spelling;
- model strategies for checking and improving spelling, syntax, and punctuation;

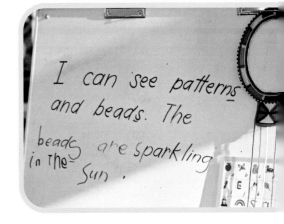

- model strategies for rereading and revising texts;
- develop students' vocabulary and their knowledge of syntax and idiom;
- show students how to choose language to convey emotion or to persuade an audience;
- demonstrate the use of a range of forms and structures in written language;
- develop students' sense of an author's purpose and of the different audiences for different types of text.

During shared writing, as the teacher prompts, gives feedback, explains, and questions, valuable conversations arise between the teacher and students and also among students. In order to encourage the ideas and contributions of all the students, the teacher may sometimes need to elicit a response from the shy or new child. Effective teachers build and maintain a momentum so that all students are motivated and engaged in the activity.

I reinforce reading and writing behaviours through shared and guided reading and writing sessions throughout the week. Each day, I tell my own story – just one sentence long. The students love hearing and reading about my dogs and other funny or sad incidents. They often suggest to me what I might write about. During the writing, I articulate my sentence, and the students repeat it and clap it, to help use the rhythm to retain the idea. I model where to begin and the spaces between the words, and I articulate words slowly, to identify the sounds we can hear.

The students say the word slowly together and may use their alphabet charts or resources around the room to help locate a sound-to-letter match or a known sight word. I select the students who I know have just mastered a concept to contribute. It might be to locate a high-frequency word, or to give me the first, middle, or last letter they can hear, or to tell me to put in a space or a full stop. This helps to reinforce and celebrate their new learning. We all reread after every word to check what we have written and establish what our next word will be. When the sentence is complete, we check: "Is this what I mean to say?" "Can I put in the full stop now?" When agreement is reached, we reread it, and the students clap to represent the full stop.

The students then discuss with a partner what they are going to write about, and they articulate their writing goal before they draw pictures as part of the process for clarifying their ideas. I focus the students on their personal goals before they begin their writing, using reminders like "Say your words slowly and write down the first and last letters that you hear" or "Use a full stop at the end of the sentence."

The students are making quite rapid progress because they are very clear about what they are paying attention to and are getting appropriate feedback.

Teacher, new entrants to year 1

A great deal of implicit learning occurs in shared writing, just as it does in language experience activities. The students listen actively and also participate as the teacher makes links to what they have recently read, heard, or written.

Teachers can introduce students to many forms of text during shared writing – reports, recounts, instructions, explanations, descriptions, narratives, charts, labels, speech balloons, wall stories, captions for photographs, diaries, shopping lists, recipes, dialogue, poetry, and more. Familiar texts can also provide starting points for shared writing. The teacher and students can innovate on a story, a poem, or even a particular sentence that they enjoyed, patterning a new idea on its style and structure. This can lead to conversations that build the students' awareness, especially when teachers model strategic questions like: "What makes this good writing?" "How can we make our writing like this?"

The teacher uses shared writing to develop the students' understanding of how different kinds of writing meet different purposes. By making links with the students' reading, teachers can elicit or explain the reasons why, for example, lists, reports, instructions, and letters are presented differently. The teacher helps the students to make the connections and to transfer the learning to their reading or future writing (see also chapter 5).

Interactive writing

In "interactive writing", a variation of shared writing, all the children are involved in scribing the common text. Each child needs a marker or pencil and a small whiteboard or clipboard. The teacher leads the writing, but all the children write down the text themselves, sometimes copying and sometimes writing known letters and words themselves.

Interactive writing is most effective with a small group. It provides a safe and supportive environment for reluctant writers, for NESB students (students from non-English-speaking backgrounds), and for any students who need to give intensive attention to features of the English language.

By involving their students in this way as "apprentices", the teacher can make explicit the various conventions of print (such as spacing, punctuation, and directionality) as well as helping the children to express meaning and think about what is being written. As the children become more confident and fluent, they will move from interactive writing, where they are fully supported, to guided writing.

I use everyday events or objects to create sentences to work with. If it's a windy day, we might discuss what it feels, sounds, or looks like, and I will draw out from the students a sentence that captures what they think, feel, or notice, like "The wind is whooing and booming". My focus is to help the students to extend their vocabulary and articulate and record a complete sentence.

I encourage them to quickly record the known words and help them to slowly articulate, hear, and record the sounds in the words that are unfamiliar to them. "You can write 'the'. Say 'wind' slowly. What can you hear?" The students independently use their knowledge of sound-to-letter relationships to attempt the unknown words on their whiteboards while being observed and prompted to make connections between what they know and what they are learning. "You can write 'in'. Now, how can you write 'wind'?" I record the correct word on my chart, and this provides instant feedback on their efforts. This way, they are receiving a correct model to read from.

Teacher, year 1 class

Using shared writing to meet diverse needs

Shared writing is an effective way of supporting NESB students. They can see the text growing slowly and carefully as the teacher scribes, and they can be encouraged, in this supportive environment, to contribute ideas. Words and phrases are repeated and revised, enabling all the students to build on their existing vocabulary and language skills. This is also very valuable for students who are experiencing difficulties in writing, including those who lack confidence or motivation.

Shared writing enables teachers to build the learning of those whose home literacy practices differ from those of the school, to incorporate these students' expertise, and to help them learn about classroom literacy activities. In shared writing, topics can be chosen to reflect the students' diverse experiences and backgrounds.

Guided writing

In guided writing, as in guided reading, the student progressively takes control of the writing process. The teacher usually works with a group on a focused task. The teacher knows what the students have already learned, what their needs and interests are, and what their next learning steps will be. These steps are generally identified as the learning goals for a writing task that follows on from a model provided during shared writing. The students construct their texts individually, working with the ideas about writing already developed with the teacher. The teacher supports them in working out how best to convey their message to the intended audience.

During guided writing sessions, students can practise any or all of the steps in the writing process (as set out on pages 138–141). The students learn from each other as well as from the teacher, seeking and responding to feedback as they each think and talk their way through the task.

The teacher's instructional objective may be to:

- teach a writing skill, for example, how to write dialogue using correct punctuation;
- focus the students' attention on a specific strategy for writing, such as using mind maps to plan a text;
- provide a framework within which individual students can develop their personal voice;
- build the students' vocabulary knowledge by using new language and clarifying it in initial discussion;
- encourage the students to choose words carefully, thinking about their likely effect on the intended audience;
- teach the students about the characteristics of different text forms;
- build in the students a sense of being one of a community of writers.

Independent writing

As well as working on teacher-directed writing tasks, students need time to write for their own purposes while engaging with topics that are significant to them.

Independent writing gives students opportunities to explore ideas that interest them and to practise what they have learned during shared and guided writing. Students need opportunities to write simply and honestly about their own experiences and things that matter a lot to them and to share their writing. Teachers provide a good model when they share their own writing and are as honest and specific in their writing as they expect their students to be.

When the students are writing on their own, the teacher can observe their writing and note their progress. Teachers should be ready to support or guide when necessary, but they need to be sensitive about intervening in a way that might interrupt a writer's train of thought or reduce their sense of ownership of their writing. Writing should always be an enjoyable activity. Students should look forward to sharing their writing with a teacher who helps them to reflect critically on what they have written and to consider how the reader will feel when reading it.

Students should always have the opportunity to share their finished writing with a group or class and to see their work displayed. The teacher models collaborative ways of talking about writing so that the students are supported in sharing their work and can help one another to extend their thinking and clarify their meaning. When everyone is involved in helping to extend a piece of writing in a supportive and creative classroom climate, all the students benefit.

Further reading

For full reference details of the resources listed here, refer to pages 189–194.

Useful resources about the effective use of instructional strategies to make a difference to students' learning include:

Anstey, M. (1998). "Being Explicit about Literacy Instruction".
Askew, S., ed. (2000). *Feedback for Learning.*
Cazden, C. B. (2001). *Classroom Discourse: The Language of Teaching and Learning.*
Clay, M. M. (1998). *By Different Paths to Common Outcomes.*
Duffy, G. G. (2002). "The Case for Direct Explanation of Strategies".
Edwards-Groves, C. (1999). "Explicit Teaching: Focusing Teacher Talk on Literacy".
McNaughton, S. (2001). "Asking the Right Questions: What Learning Do We Value and What Contexts Enable That Learning?"

Texts on strategies for literacy teaching in schools with students from diverse cultural and linguistic backgrounds (with a particular focus on Māori and Pasifika students) include:

Bishop, R. and Glynn, T. (2000). "Kaupapa Māori Messages for the Mainstream".
Education Review Office (2002). *Māori Students: Schools Making a Difference.*
Glynn, T., Atvars, K., and O'Brien, K (1999). *Culturally Appropriate Strategies for Assisting Māori Students Experiencing Learning and Behavioural Difficulties.*
McNaughton, S. (2002). *Meeting of Minds.*
Phillips, G., McNaughton, S., and MacDonald, S. (2000). *Picking up the Pace: Effective Literacy Interventions for Accelerated Progress over the Transition into Decile 1 Schools.*
Tuafuti, P. (1997). "Teaching Practices for Bilingual Classrooms: Which Are Most Successful?"
Turoa, L., Wolfgramm, E., Tanielu, L., and McNaughton, S. (2002). *Pathways over the Transition to Schools: Studies in Family Literacy Practices and Effective Classroom Contexts for Māori and Pasifika Children.*

Further resources that discuss strategies for teaching reading and writing include:

Anderson, K. (2001). *Motivating the Reluctant Writer.*
Hood, H. (1997). *Left to Write Too.*
Ministry of Education (1993). *Reciprocal Teaching: Extending Reading Strategies.*
Ministry of Education (1992). *Dancing with the Pen.*
Ministry of Education (1996a). *Exploring Language: A Handbook for Teachers.*
Ministry of Education (1996b). *The Learner as a Reader: Developing Reading Programmes.*
Ministry of Education (1997b). *Reading and Beyond: Discovering Language through Ready to Read.*
Ministry of Education (2001b). *Ready to Read Teacher Support Material: Emergent Level.*
Ministry of Education (2002b). *Ready to Read Teacher Support Material: Early Levels.*
Parkes, B. (2002). *Read It Again! Revisiting Shared Reading.*
Smith, J. and Elley, W. (1997a). *How Children Learn to Read.*
Smith, J. and Elley, W. (1997b). *How Children Learn to Write.*
Thompson, L. M. (2002). *Guided Reading: Years 1–4.*

Chapter 5:

Engaging Learners with Texts

Introduction

Text is defined in this book as a piece of connected, meaningful writing. Although this book focuses on written forms, texts also exist, and can be created, in oral and visual forms.

Engaging learners with texts means placing the use and creation of texts at the heart of literacy learning.

Effective literacy teaching practice involves using texts to engage students in their reading and supporting the students as they create texts in their writing.

In perhaps more than any other way, teachers make a difference to students' learning through providing rich experiences with texts. Often a breakthrough in a student's progress will be the unlocking of a book that inspires them or the discovery that they can write something that others want to read. The value of the sense of achievement and confidence that such a moment brings cannot be overestimated and will stand the student in good stead in their subsequent years at school, when increasing demands on their literacy competence will be made across the curriculum.

There is convincing evidence that engaging students in rich experiences with texts has a strong positive impact on student achievement. Studies show that:

• using and creating texts is a key way to motivate students, and motivation promotes learning;

• vocabulary built through rich-text activities enhances students' achievement, for example, in comprehension;

• experiences with texts that have different forms and structures are associated with positive student outcomes;

• opportunities for many reading and writing experiences are associated with student achievement.

This chapter discusses and gives examples of teachers' effective use of text-based activities in the three aspects (see page 24) of the framework for describing literacy acquisition: learning the code, making meaning, and thinking critically.

The reciprocal nature of reading and writing

Talking and listening are the two sides of spoken communication, and reading and writing are just as closely linked. Readers and writers use their knowledge and experience: readers to construct meaning from text and writers to construct meaning in text. The reader interacts with letters and words in text in order to construct meaning; the writer starts with ideas and represents these in letters and words and in the appropriate form and style. To communicate in written language successfully, learners need to read like writers and to write like readers. They learn that both reading and writing are purposeful, express meaning, share the same functions, and use the same print conventions. In setting their instructional objectives, teachers need to plan to make students aware of these links.

As they write their ideas, students draw on the same basic knowledge about print and use the same sources of information as when reading. For example, both readers and writers need to be aware of:

- the one-to-one relationship between spoken and written words;
- the match between the sequence of the sounds in spoken and in written language;
- the fact that a piece of text says the same thing each time it is read;
- the fact that the structure of English determines the order of words in a sentence.

In order to encode accurately and make sense in their writing, students need to self-monitor, detect errors, and self-correct, just as they do in reading.

Studies of effective teachers have shown[42] that they continually make explicit the connections between reading and writing. Teachers who have a grasp of this reciprocal relationship recognise that writing is neither secondary to reading nor something to be taught separately from reading.

---

[42] Refer to Pressley, Allington, Wharton-McDonald, Block, and Morrow (2001).

A range and variety of texts

There are a number of reasons why it is important that students and teachers make use of a range and variety of texts for reading and writing.

- In any classroom, the students' developmental pathways vary and their values and perspectives are diverse.
- Teachers use a range of instructional strategies and approaches to meet their objectives as they teach students to decode and encode, make meaning, and think critically. In the process, they use many different kinds of texts as examples and models.
- Students need many opportunities to practise reading and writing and to reinforce their learning through using and creating a variety of texts.
- In order to foster independent and recreational reading and writing, teachers need to offer plenty of variety and guide students towards selecting widely. Students need to learn to read and write many different kinds of text for different purposes and audiences.

The variety of the texts that students read and write can be considered in terms of:

- their topic or theme;
- their purpose and form;
- their intended audience;
- their literary style;
- the writer's perspective;
- their instructional reading level;
- the medium they are presented through.

The growing range of quality New Zealand texts, both fiction and non-fiction, is a great resource for teachers and students. Teachers should provide students with texts that present authentic Māori perspectives and also those of Pasifika communities and other groups that are part of New Zealand's diverse society. Literary classics – memorable texts that help children understand themselves and their world – often have a lasting impact. The range should include other materials as well as stories, such as tables, diagrams and maps, poetry, reference texts, readalong audio resources, email messages, and Internet websites. It should also include picture books at all levels. These resources not only foster students' reading: they also inspire their writing.[43]

---

[43] Refer to pages 94–135 of *The Learner as a Reader* for a detailed discussion of a wide range of text forms and how they can be used.

The value of reading and writing non-fiction texts is sometimes underestimated. A non-fiction topic can provide a "hook" to arouse interest or motivate a student who is experiencing difficulties in their literacy learning. The focus of most children's early literacy experiences is on narrative forms but, for later success, they need to learn to use texts and reference sources for content area reading and writing. It is important for teachers to have clear instructional objectives for engaging their students with a range of non-fiction texts.[44]

Students need to engage with texts in a variety of media. Electronic media, when used purposefully and integrated into classroom activities, give learners many opportunities for problem solving and creative thinking and offer choices for composing and presenting texts. Teachers need to help students using the Internet to develop the knowledge and strategies they need in order to locate material, evaluate its usefulness, accuracy, and authenticity, and distinguish fact from opinion.

The range of material that can be accessed and composed through electronic media, especially the Internet, makes it increasingly important for students to be able to make informed judgments about the electronic texts they use. For writers using multimedia modes, the range of choices for presenting texts is enormous; writers need an understanding of how different modes affect readers. The forms and content of the mass media, including television, music, film, pictures, signs, and sculptures, also influence students' literacy development. Students need to become discerning users of language in many forms.

[44] Refer to *Guided Reading: Years 1–4*, pages 35–38.

Meeting many needs

Teachers face a challenge in planning reading and writing activities to meet many needs. Every student has unique needs, and some groups of students have particular needs. Such groups include:

- new learners of English;
- rapid-progress students, who need to be extended;
- students from backgrounds with literacy practices that differ from the conventional practices of the school;
- students experiencing difficulties in literacy learning.

Many factors – for example, the choice of topic for writing and the balance, factual accuracy, and authenticity of texts for reading – affect whether students become motivated and engaged in text activities. Students who can identify closely with what they meet in text activities are likely to engage better with the task.

It is sound practice at any time to incorporate into learning activities what is valuable and familiar to the learner. This is particularly the case in using and creating texts, given the positive impact that text-based experiences have on students' achievement. Teachers need to actively seek ways to incorporate the practices and perspectives of all their students, for example, by selecting texts and writing tasks that reflect all students' cultural values. This is an essential element of teachers' diversity awareness (see page 46).

There are many effective ways for a teacher to make links between the home and school contexts of children's learning in ways that are visible to and significant for the child. Literacy teaching can be made more effective for Māori and Pasifika children, for example, by incorporating familiar content into classroom practices and building on some of the relevant practices that children bring with them to school. Teachers may:

- use texts or plan writing activities with themes that reflect the cultural values and perspectives of Māori or Pasifika students (see the examples on pages 91, 99, and 103);
- build on Pasifika children's expertise in recitation, developed through church and family literacy practices, by including recitation among classroom activities;
- build on the Māori concept of the tuakana-teina relationship (see page 164);
- build relationships in the classroom that make for peer collaboration in using and creating texts.

Students from non-English-speaking backgrounds (NESB students) have some particular literacy learning needs. Teachers should encourage NESB students and their families to use their first language as a foundation on which to build the students' knowledge of English. Learning to read in their first language supports a child in achieving success with reading in a second language.[45] However, NESB children will differ in their strengths in using their first languages and in the English-language strengths that they bring to school, so teachers need to look at each child's needs when planning text-based activities.

It should not be assumed that a child who does not yet speak English fluently needs to have their literacy instruction delayed or limited to lower level skills and surface features of texts. Like all learners, NESB students need many rich experiences with texts from the outset. It's helpful to provide texts in their first language as well as English.

NESB students have to learn a whole range of new concepts and skills in English – a far more complex and challenging task than just learning to speak a language. For younger learners … it is critical that first-language maintenance goes on at home and is supported in the school and in the home. Not only will continued development in the first language provide a bridge, allowing cognitive development to continue while English is being learned, but it is also likely to have a significant impact on the NESB student's self-concept, confidence, and attitude.

Non-English-Speaking-Background Students: A Handbook for Schools, page 19

---

[45] Refer to Braunger and Lewis (1998) and Snow and RAND Reading Study Group (2001).

A classroom-based intervention

Analysis of assessment data has indicated that a group of eight children in my class (four of them NESB students) are having difficulty hearing and recording sounds, particularly medial vowels and word endings. All their efforts during independent writing are taken up in getting the words onto the page. I want them to be freed up to think about the message, build a writing vocabulary, and see themselves as writers.

During the first four weeks of this term, I am engaging this group for about five minutes each day in a focused writing session. These writing sessions have a five-day cycle. On Monday, the children and I jointly construct a sentence, basing it on something topical in the classroom. Last Monday's sentence, "We can find frogs in spring, living in still water", links to our current science topic. The sentence is also used for handwriting practice on the first day. I also make links during guided reading to the words or letter sequences that the children are learning. On subsequent days, I scaffold new sound-letter information in the sentence as the children write. "You know the 'ing' sound, it's the same as in 'trying'." I articulate clearly while the children are recording and focus on any letter-sound confusions that the NESB children have. As the children gain mastery of the learning, we add one or two sentences during the week. On Wednesday, we added "Frogs can leap", so that we could focus on the long "ea" sound in "leap".

Each day, I share back the correct model, and each child marks their own work, deciding what they are going to concentrate on getting correct the next day. By Friday, the pace has built up, and the children swap their writing with a peer, who marks it. Then they talk to their partner about one thing they could do differently the following week, and this becomes the child's goal. I note and give feedback on these goals when conferencing with each child.

Already I can see the impact of this short, focused activity, during shared writing and in their independent writing. Their hearing of sounds is improving, and this is leading to greater fluency in getting their message down. Their spelling is improving; they are developing a wider writing vocabulary and are using explicit language to talk about their writing. The children are highly motivated because the context is meaningful to them. They are experiencing success, getting explicit written feedback, and reflecting on their learning. They are gaining greater confidence in themselves as writers.

Teacher, years 1 to 3

A focus on purpose

In order to engage learners in a reading or writing activity, teachers need to be clear about:

- what they want the students to learn (the teacher's instructional objective, which is based on the identified needs of the learners);
- how they will share this intended learning with the students (the shared goal);
- what the task will be and which instructional strategies will be most effective;
- how they and the students will know that the learning has taken place (for example, through shared success criteria and through monitoring and reflection).

When teachers are explicit in sharing with students the reasons for a reading or writing task, they give point to the task and build the expectation that reading and writing will always be for a purpose. By reviewing the purpose and reflecting on the learning at the end of the activity, they reinforce this expectation.

Engaging Learners with Texts

Identifying learners' needs

Setting instructional objectives
- Learning the code
- Making meaning
- Thinking critically

Planning literacy activities

*Strategic decisions about literacy activities
are made with regard to:*

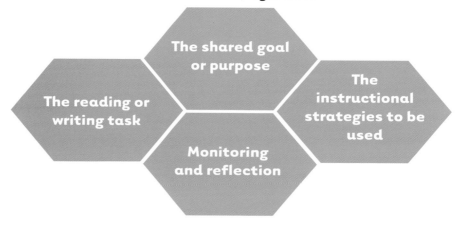

The shared goal
or purpose

The reading or
writing task

The
instructional
strategies to be
used

Monitoring
and reflection

*With teacher support,
students develop knowledge and strategies
and awareness of how to use them.*

Knowing texts

To meet their instructional objectives and provide their students with varied, interesting, and enjoyable reading and writing experiences, teachers need a detailed knowledge of the forms and features of texts. With such knowledge, they can plan activities through which the students learn and practise decoding and encoding, making meaning, and thinking critically.

Teachers who are familiar with the features of texts for reading, and with their potential for use in many contexts and for many purposes, can use texts to maximum effect.[46] Teachers should also ensure that students learn to write for a wide range of purposes and in many forms.[47]

Rich texts

Texts for reading may be described as rich when they:

- motivate and challenge students as readers;
- relate to students' interests or arouse their interest;
- are enjoyable and informative;
- draw on and affirm the social and cultural identities of the students in the classroom;
- use appropriate language (in terms of how complex it is and also in terms of how familiar readers will be with the way the language is used);
- encourage thoughtful responses.

Students are likely to create rich texts when the texts that they write:

- arise from the students' interests, experiences, or needs;
- motivate and challenge the students as writers;
- have a purpose;
- draw on and affirm the social and cultural identities of the students in the classroom;
- provide the students with opportunities to use appropriate language to give written form to their own voices;
- encourage thoughtfulness in the writing process;
- are planned to have an impact on the audience.

Examples of rich texts for reading are provided on pages 122-125, and examples of rich texts that students have written are provided on pages 125-126.

---

[46] Guidance is provided in the *Ready to Read Teacher Support Material* and the *School Journal Teachers' Notes.*

[47] The New Zealand exemplars for writing give detailed guidance about purpose and form and about the surface features and deeper features of students' writing at different levels.

Mum's Octopus

This is an example of a rich text[48] that invites multiple uses. Depending on their identified needs, the learners' focus could be on any of the following points.

- A well-constructed narrative that provides a model of the story form and is well paced to hold attention, with moments of drama, such as:
  - the octopus fastening onto Mum's arm
  - the interchange before they release the octopus

- Family life: family activities, doing things together, and the warmth illustrated in the picture of the larger family group on the last page

- Affirming and valuing cultural identity; gathering seafood is a family activity familiar to many Pasifika students and students from other cultural groups

- Many opportunities for deeper thinking and rich discussion, including the sharing of points of view (What would you have done? Why? What would be the effect on the other family members?)

- The humour and irony, for example:
  - on page 5, "Don't let go" when the octopus had a firm hold of Mum
  - on page 9, "Who caught it?" when it had, in fact, caught Mum

- Character development within the space of a brief narrative

- Relationships of mother and father, father and son

- The resolution at the end and the child's role in this

- Some special moments for predicting and inferring, for example, on page 8

- Opportunities to develop comprehension strategies:
  - inferring
  - hypothesising
  - empathising
  - making connections

- Rich variety in vocabulary, sentence structure, and use of language:
  - challenges such as "octopus" and "tentacles"
  - colloquial language, for example, "a good feed"
  - descriptive verbs; irregular verbs; doubling of consonants for past tense
  - contractions

- Effective use of dialogue to carry the action forward and to convey point of view or emotion

- The brilliant way the illustrations enhance the narrative

- Perspectives in the illustrations:
  - on page 5, the way the octopus is clinging, dominant in the picture
  - on page 8, the octopus in the bucket
  - on page 10, the way it is shooting away in the green ocean
  - on pages 4 and 9, the tilting horizon

---

[48] *Mum's Octopus* by D. Long (illustrations by Gus Sinaumea Hunter)

- The expressions on people's faces and the body language of each member of the family (what is each thinking, for example, on page 8, when looking at the octopus, and on page 10, when the octopus is released?)

- Links across the curriculum for literacy learning in:
  - science: the sea shore, creatures of rock pools, tidal zones
  - health and physical education: safety issues for people near the sea, family relationships and activities, group decision making.

The text provides rich models for students' own writing and for oral and visual language activities. Refer also to the ideas in the *Ready to Read Teacher Support Material* for using this title.

"Wow, that was cool, Mum," said Sione.
Mum looked at her arm
to see if there were any marks.
Then everyone looked in the bucket.
The octopus looked back.

"I'm not eating that," said Mum.
"I'm letting it go."
"You can't," said Dad. "That's our dinner."
He was shocked.
"Who caught it?" asked Mum.

9

Mum carried the bucket over to a rock pool
and tipped the octopus out.
She watched it shoot away through the water.
Dad sighed.

10

123

Kaz was belaying. This means that the rope attached to Hemisha's harness went up to the top of the wall, threaded through a metal clip called a karabiner, and then came back down and was attached to Kaz's harness.

As Hemisha climbed, Kaz pulled the rope tight. If Hemisha slipped, she would dangle from the rope, but she wouldn't fall to the ground.

10

"Freaky!"

This text[49] is one of many *School Journal* articles that are a rich resource for literacy teaching and learning. It has the appeal – and the challenges – of a magazine style presentation, which is popular among more experienced readers who are looking for variety and range in what they read. As outlined below, "Freaky!" has many of the characteristics that invite readers to revisit a text. It can be used to meet many instructional objectives, including objectives that are intended to develop students' comprehension strategies and critical thinking. This article provides:

- an example of a narrative that:
  - is on a high-interest topic, with the spice of danger
  - is enjoyable and motivating, having the authenticity of an actual event
  - has emotional impact – children's feelings are captured in their personal responses as they admit their fear and savour their achievement
  - contains a range of challenges in language, structure, and concepts
  - is complemented by photographs that provide informative detail and perspective
  - is presented using visually interesting typefaces, especially on the last page;

- a context for deeper thinking and rich discussion, for example, about:
  - why we choose to do something that is scary (making links to children's own experiences of facing up to something difficult and how they felt afterwards)
  - what would happen if a member of the class didn't want to do it
  - that it's OK to say you're scared;

- variety in language use, vocabulary, and sentence structure, for example:
  - language that conveys emotion, such as "freaked" and "awesome"
  - use of connectors, such as "first", "next", and "then"
  - technical terms that are supported and explained within the narrative;

- a model (in form and content) for the students' own writing, for example, writing about personal experience, poetic writing, recounts, descriptions, and explanations;

- information that could lead to the students' undertaking research, for example, on rock climbing or other outdoor adventure activities.

---

[49] "Freaky!" by J. Cooper

Links across the curriculum include:

- science:
  - the principle of pulleys, "over vertical" and "under vertical" surfaces
  - equipment: helmet and harness;
- health and physical education:
  - the technique for coming down the wall
  - meeting challenge, overcoming fear
  - equipment, and adult supervision and assurance
  - following instructions for safety and success
  - meeting challenge, courage
  - teamwork ("Everyone cheered"), the class as a supportive community.

The following three examples of students' writing are among *The New Zealand Curriculum Exemplars* for English (see page 192 for reference details). This example is of a student's writing at level 1i.

My Dad Has the Same Shoes

Nathan has recalled specific features about his dad that are prominent in his mind. He has presented these facts as a personal and endearing statement about his dad.

Deeper features

Voice
Records simple and honest observation of character.

Ideas
Has something to say about a character.

Sentences
Attempts a compound sentence.

Vocabulary
Uses appropriate content words.

Language features
Focuses on physical description but also includes a specific feature.

Student's first draft

my Dab has the sam shos as em and has kr/o here

curly

hair

My Dab has the sam shos as em and has Krle here

[My dad has the same shoes as me and has curly hair.]

Surface features

Spelling
Attempts to use initial letter sounds, including a digraph.

Approximates common spellings.

Spells some high-frequency words correctly.

Punctuation
Beginning to use capital letters.

Grammar
Sentence makes sense.

Layout
Leaves spaces between words.

Demonstrates directionality.

These are examples of students' writing at levels 1iii (Ryan) and 2 (Benji).

Why Do We Wear Our Seatbelt?

Ryan expresses strong personal reasons for wearing seatbelts. This is explained clearly in simple, precise language.

Deeper features

Impact
Explains a personally significant occurrence with some clarity.

Ideas
Includes ideas and reasons, mostly subjective, and supported by some simple detail.

Sentences
Uses mainly simple sentences with variation in beginnings.

Structure
Defines topic through opening question and answer.

Uses simple cause-and-effect words to support ideas.

Vocabulary
Uses high-frequency words and some key content words.

Student's second draft

Why do we wear our Seatbget seatbelt in the car? We wear our seat Seatbelt because we will break the Law. If we don't wear our seatbelt we will get pilled over by a policeman He will tell toll you to give him some money. Your Seatbelt pulls you back when you have a carcrash.

Surface features

Grammar
Writes a simple sentence correctly.

Spelling
Shows good knowledge of basic spelling patterns.

Punctuation
Uses capital letters and full stops with some consistency.

> Why do we wear our seatbelt in the car? We wear our seatbelt because we will break the Law. If we don't wear our seatbelt we will get pilled over by a policeman. He will tell you to give him some money. Your seatbelt pulls you back when you have a carcrash.

If There Were No Cats

In writing to the Prime Minister on the topic of whether cats should be banned in New Zealand, Benji knows exactly whom he wants to persuade. He attempts to play on his reader's emotions, and supports his argument with elements of personal experience.

Deeper features

Ideas
Presents ideas with some supporting evidence: "because ...".

Structure
Begins to sequence ideas.

Sentences
Varies beginnings.

Attempts complex sentences.

Vocabulary
Makes increasing use of topic-related vocabulary.

Language features
Attempts rhetorical questions.

Student's second draft

Dear prime Minister
I am writing about your suggest law: that cats should be banned from New Zealand.

I disagree with you because you don't need to bannd cats from the hole of New Zealand just from one city like Auckland or crischrch Cats ant the only problem. there a miner problem. Wher would childrin lern risponsiblity from if ther were no cats.

If there were no cats who would play with old womans wollin balls and who would grand mas snugl up to in their big rocking cher

You can't banned them. there to cute, fuzz and helples.

Surface features

Grammar
Attempts more complex sentences.

Spelling
Shows knowledge of consonant sounds: crischrch, snugl, lern.

> Dear prime Minister
> I am writing about your suggest law: that cats should be banned from New Zealand.
>
> I disagree with you because you don't need to bannd cats from the hole of New Zealand just from one city like Auckland or Crischrch. Cats ant the only problem there a miner problem. Wher would childrin lern risponsibility from if ther were no cats.
>
> If there were no cats who would play with old womons wollin balls and who would grandmas snugl up to in their big rocking cher
>
> You can't banned them there to cute, fuzz and helples.

A note on text difficulty in reading

Text difficulty or level is usefully thought of as getting an appropriate balance between supports and challenges. Supports are the features of text that make it easy to read, and challenges are the potential difficulties, *for particular readers*. It's important to remember that supports and challenges exist only in relation to the reader: what one student finds a challenge, another may find a support. The appropriate difficulty level of a text depends on many factors, including:

- the students' prior knowledge of and interest in the content;
- the range and complexity of the vocabulary;
- the students' sight vocabulary and their current decoding competence;
- the layout of the text, including line length and word spacing;
- the support given by the illustrations;
- the length of the text;
- the syntax of the text and the complexity and length of the sentences;
- the number and nature of new ideas or concepts presented in the text.

The teacher will choose texts at different levels for different purposes, for instance, when reading to the children, using the book as a shared text, giving instruction during guided reading, or providing books for students' independent or recreational reading.

Most published series of texts for teaching reading are arranged in a gradient of difficulty. These gradients are generally a good guide, especially when they have been developed, like the Ready to Read levels, in consultation with practising teachers. But there is no formula or set levelling sequence that determines the "readability" of a text or the order in which texts should be used. The teacher, who knows the learners and their needs and interests, makes the decisions.

Using texts

Developing readers' processing strategies

Teachers have a crucial role in helping their students to develop a network of reading strategies and awareness of how to use them. Providing rich experiences of purposeful reading, using an expanding range of texts, is central to this development. The examples on pages 128–130 show how teachers can give instruction that is both strategic and explicit when working with students as they develop these essential strategies. The emphasis may initially be on decoding and making sense, but thinking critically about the text is part of reading and writing from the beginning of instruction – the aspects develop together. Above all, the activities should be motivating and enjoyable for all students.

Attending and searching

Learners need to attend to details of text in order to decode and determine meaning. The learner looks purposefully for particular information, for known letters, clusters, or words, for familiar text features and patterns of syntax, and for information in pictures and diagrams.

For beginning readers, this usually involves attending closely to every word (especially to the initial letters of words) and to the illustrations.

For fluent readers, this usually involves taking in larger chunks of text (phrases rather than words) and slowing down to identify and focus on specific words or features only when necessary to clarify meaning.

With instruction from the teacher, learners begin to acquire a sight vocabulary and to develop understandings about text. They learn to focus more effectively, attending to what is relevant at the time in order to get the message. Teachers provide specific instruction to help them to draw on what they know and can do. Attending and searching may involve the learner in doing some or all of the following.

What learners do	*How teachers prompt and support*
• focus attention on particular letters or letter clusters and draw on what they know about letter-sound relationships • identify the words they already know • look for information in illustrations and diagrams • use analogies – that is, use their knowledge of familiar words (can, get) to work out new words (man, ran, pan; let, set, pet).	Tell me the first sound of this word. ("sunhat", page 6) What letter does this word start with? ("dad", page 7) What do you notice about the last letter in "dad"? That's right. It's the same as the first letter. Which words do you know on this page? Who can you see in this picture? (page 7) Which word is different on this page? What do you notice about this word? ("sunhat", page 6 – a compound word)

Here is my sunhat.

6

Here is my dad.

7

This example features *Let's Go* by Feana Tu'akoi, photographs by Mark Round, Ready to Read series, Learning Media, 2001.

Predicting

Predicting is a strategy that readers use not only to identify words but also to anticipate what might come next. It involves forming an expectation on the basis of the information acquired so far, so it is strongly related to meaning and is more than speculation. Predictions draw on readers' prior knowledge and their use of syntactic, semantic, and visual and grapho-phonic information in the text.

For beginning readers, predicting is usually at the level of individual words. For example, learners use their knowledge of letter-sound relationships to identify the initial sound of a word, or they draw on the pattern of a repetitive text to support them in working out what might happen next. Beginning readers often rely a great deal on the illustrations.

For fluent readers, predicting involves using prior knowledge and information in the text quickly, and usually automatically, to decide (at least initially) on the meaning of unknown words or difficult passages or to anticipate, for example, the next event in a narrative or the next step in an argument.

As learners become familiar with patterns of sentences, book language, and basic text structures, they build their ability to use prediction.

Teachers need to explicitly teach beginning readers to predict unknown words and show them exactly how to predict what will come next in a text. Predicting may involve the learner in doing some or all of the following.

What learners do

- draw on their letter-sound knowledge
- draw on their awareness of the patterns of text
- sound out the word or parts of the word and use meaning and syntax to narrow the possibilities
- focus on a detail in an illustration or diagram
- repeat or rerun the preceding text and sound out the first letter
- use their prior knowledge to predict what a character might do next or what the next step in an argument might be.

This example features *The Praying Mantis* by Pauline Cartwright, photographs by Nic Bishop, Ready to Read series, Learning Media, 1993.

How teachers prompt and support

Read that again. What sound does the word start with?

What would make sense?

What could you try?

What sound do these letters make?

What's happening in the picture on page 4?

What will the fly do now? Has it noticed the praying mantis?

That's right. The fly comes b...

What do you think will happen next?

A fly goes by.

The fly comes back.

4

Cross-checking, confirming, and self-correcting

Teachers need to show beginning readers how to monitor their own reading. The reader needs to cross-check predictions to ensure that they make sense and fit with other information already processed. When children detect or suspect an error, they need to have strategies to fix it. For example, a beginning reader may notice that there is a mismatch between what they have read and what is in the picture or in the print. Noticing the problem is the first step; knowing what to do to fix it is the next. Readers cross-check by drawing on their prior knowledge and on the syntactic, semantic, and visual and grapho-phonic information in the text. Cross-checking often involves turning a partially correct response into a correct one.

For beginning readers, cross-checking usually involves checking that their prediction of an individual word fits and makes sense. Their checking and confirming often take time and are quite deliberate.

For fluent readers, cross-checking usually involves further searching for information to confirm their initial understanding. In skilled reading, predictions are usually checked swiftly and automatically.

As readers progress, they learn that cross-checking, confirming, and self-correcting are among the habits of a good reader and take responsibility for using these strategies. Cross-checking, confirming, and self-correcting may involve the learner in doing some or all of the following.

How teachers prompt and support

Does that look right? If the word was "called", what would you expect to see at the end/in the middle?

You said, "There is a hole in my sock." Check the first word again. Look at the end of the word.

You said "make". Does that make sense? Could that be "menders"? How do you know?

What did you notice [after a hesitation or pause]?

How do you know for sure?

You're so clever. How did you know that?

Read the whole sentence. Does that sound right to you?

Something wasn't quite right. Try that again.

How did you know what was wrong?

This example features *The Hole in the King's Sock* by Dot Meharry, illustrated by Philip Webb, Ready to Read series, Learning Media, 2001.

What learners do

- draw on the meaning or pattern of the text and use illustrations and word knowledge to check and confirm their prediction
- reread a word, phrase, or sentence
- use their knowledge of spoken language or book language to decide whether the piece of text "sounds right"
- think about the meaning of what they are reading.

The King had cold feet.
He looked at his socks.
"There's a hole in my sock!" he cried.
"Get me the Royal Menders."

The Royal Menders came running.
"We will mend the hole
in your sock," they said.
They stitched the hole
in the King's sock with gold thread.

Helping learners to use the range of strategies

The strategies are not used individually but in combination, and learners need explicit instruction in how to select and integrate them. Through monitoring learners' processing of text, the teacher can identify the strategies they are using and show them how to use the whole range. For example, teachers can:

- model the effective use of different strategies in the context of a wide range of texts;
- ask learners how they arrived at a solution and discuss the appropriate use of strategies;
- ensure that all learners have opportunities to meet challenges in texts that require them to use their repertoire of strategies to work things out for themselves;
- give informative feedback when learners find appropriate ways of solving problems.

Through such experiences, learners will have opportunities to enjoy the sense of satisfaction and success that comes when they solve their own problems and will become confident in their use of strategies.

Building comprehension

Students need to develop strategies that they can use deliberately and purposefully to enhance their understanding of text and develop their critical awareness.

While it is useful to consider comprehension strategies individually, readers do not use them separately but in complex combinations, which become increasingly complex as readers progress. Text activities based on shared goals enable students to acquire and practise these strategies. Goals for this purpose could include:

- identifying the sequence of the facts in a piece;
- describing the use of a certain kind of language in a text;
- explaining how parts of a story or procedural text relate to each other;
- describing how characters develop in a text;
- identifying the author's intention;
- identifying the purpose of the text and its structure or form.

Comprehension strategies

Making connections

Helping students to make connections between what they know and what they are reading improves their comprehension. Teachers can model making such connections, and prompt students to make links with their own knowledge and experience, when they are introducing and discussing texts for reading and in writing and oral-language activities. When activating students' prior knowledge for a particular purpose, teachers can help the students to predict, infer, and build their own interpretations as they read.

Comprehension strategies are specific, learned procedures that foster active, competent, self-regulated, and intentional reading.

Trabasso and Bouchard, 2002, page 177

131

Forming and testing hypotheses about texts

A hypothesis about a text is an expectation or opinion that the reader forms about the text before reading it. The reader then tests and revises this as they encounter and act upon new information. Hypotheses are formed on the basis of what can be discovered about the text before the content reading begins: this may include the cover, the title, the opening section, and the illustrations, and it also includes what the reader brings to the text. Depending on the goal for the task, a hypothesis may relate to the plot or character development (in a narrative) or to the conclusion of an argument. The hypothesis often takes the form of a question. The teacher can usefully model hypothesising when introducing a text and can encourage the students to seek and give feedback about their own hypotheses.

Asking questions

As in any activity, formulating questions should be directed towards a goal or intended outcome. In comprehension development, questioning helps to reinforce the habit of reading for a purpose. The teacher needs to help the students to formulate appropriate questions, for example, by modelling such questions during shared reading or writing. Asking questions helps readers to engage with the ideas in the text and with the author and gives focus to the reading task. After their reading, it's useful to help the students to evaluate the effectiveness of the questions they posed for themselves and to give them feedback for further learning.

Creating mental images or visualising

The ability to visualise or picture what is happening within a text draws readers into the text and helps them to achieve greater understanding. Studies have indicated that creating an image in the memory helps the reader to retain what is read and use it later on.[50]

Readers experiencing difficulties often need help with creating mental images and may not realise how this can help their comprehension. Asking questions such as "What picture do you see in your head?" and sharing responses will support students. It sometimes helps to have students make a sketch.

Inferring

Inferring means using content in a text, together with existing knowledge, to come to a personal conclusion about something that is not stated explicitly in the text. When the author provides clues but not all the information, we read "between the lines" to make predictions, revise these, understand underlying themes, hypothesise, make critical judgments, and draw conclusions. Inferring involves synthesising information, sometimes quite simply and sometimes at complex levels.

Teachers can help students to make inferences by asking inferential questions during shared reading or during discussion in guided reading. Or teachers may pause, when reading a text with students, to draw out clues from the text and prompt the students to make connections between different parts of the text in order to reach a conclusion.

---

[50] Refer to Trabasso and Bouchard (2002) and to Gambrell and Koskinen (2002).

Identifying the author's purpose and point of view

It is important for readers to recognise that behind every text is an author, that the author has a reason for writing, and that the reader has a reason for reading.

The purpose of the author may be to:

- provide or obtain information;
- share the excitement of an event;
- persuade or influence;
- create or enter a personal world;
- stimulate the imagination;
- convey important cultural stories or myths;
- express or appreciate a point of view.

By supporting students in discussing the purpose and point of view of a text, teachers can help them to recognise that writers bring their own experiences and concerns to their writing. Such activities contribute richly to students' awareness of the functions of texts and of how authors position readers; they also help students to build the habit of responding thoughtfully to what they read. Students then carry their new awareness to their own writing and learn to plan and articulate their specific purposes for writing as they consider purpose and point of view.

Identifying and summarising main ideas

Identifying and summarising main ideas can help students build knowledge and awareness of how texts are structured and how ideas within a text are related. Identifying the main idea or ideas in a text can present a challenge for readers. Not every text provides a neat hierarchy or clear sequence of ideas. To identify a text's most significant points, students often need to retrieve information and summarise it. They may also need to use other strategies, such as inferring the text's purpose. Teachers can show students how to identify and clarify the main points in a text by modelling how to formulate questions – for example, during in-depth discussion of a text in guided reading or when helping students to form intentions in their writing.

Analysing and synthesising

When students take apart a text they have read, examine it from their own viewpoint, and put it back together again, they make it their own. This helps them to remember what they have read and transfer what they have learned. They may feel empathy towards a character, be excited by events or information, or enjoy the style of the writing. They integrate or synthesise their newly acquired understandings and attitudes with their existing view of the world to make a new and slightly different world picture. The ways in which a reader analyses and interprets text and synthesises ideas are affected by that reader's prior knowledge, experiences, and cultural values.

Evaluating ideas and information

Good readers make a personal, informed response to a text. They not only understand the information in the text but can also generalise from it and make judgments about it in the light of what they already know. They examine and evaluate the ideas in the text and may consequently go on to confirm, extend, or change their personal views; or they may disagree with the content of a text or find an argument unconvincing.

I was discussing "Swallowed by the Sea"[51] with a group of students. We had read and discussed it for meaning the previous day – now we were reading and discussing it for the impact of its language. I wanted to link it closely to the students' own pieces of mood writing. I posed the question: "How does the author convey the atmosphere of the storm to the reader?"

Teacher	Read the first section of the story again, to see if you can create an image of the storm in your mind. What does the storm look and sound like?
Andrew	(after reading) I think it's really rough and nasty and cold.
Teacher	I agree. Let's see if we can all work out why Andrew thinks this. What clues does the author give us?
Amanda	She uses strong words in the paragraph – like "creaks" and "slap" and "pelting". They're exactly the sounds I can hear when I'm snuggled up in my bed, listening to the wind and rain outside.
Teacher	Good. Just like the main character in this story lies snuggled up in her bed. I'm pleased you've picked up on strong verbs because we've noticed them in other stories, haven't we?
Andrew	I think the author is conveying the atmosphere earlier than that. I think the first clue is when it says that the girl's breath makes a ghost on the window. I get a really cold picture in my mind from that.
Teacher	What gives you that?
Andrew	Because ghosts are all white and that makes me think of freezing cold.
Teacher	I can see some strong clues in the second paragraph as well. I can feel the wind really strongly in that paragraph. What part do you think gives me this feeling?
Hana	"The house is being sucked up and spat out."
Teacher	You're right. But what picture does that sentence create?
Hana	The wind is so strong that it can suck up something as big as a house.
Amanda	And it spits it out, just like really heavy rain spits out water all over the place.
Teacher	Great. I hope you're picking up lots of ideas for your own writing.

Teacher, year 4 class

---

[51] "Swallowed by the Sea" by A. Jackson

With a group of six children, I read Island to Island[52] *as a shared text. I wanted the children to think more deeply about their responses to text, and so the focus was higher-order thinking – hypothesising, inferring, synthesising, evaluating. I posed this question: "What are the good points and bad points about travelling to school by bus and boat?" After initially thinking this would be a fun thing to do, the children engaged in a focused discussion about some of the possible issues. The children set and maintained the initiative in the following discussion.*

Emeli	What would happen if James was sick at school and wanted to go home?
Tayla	His dad might have to take the boat all the way around the other island. You couldn't just sail over unless you had a car somewhere on the other side.
Grayson	You couldn't be late in the morning. The bus has to go a long way. It's much too far to walk. If your dad dropped you off in the boat and thought the bus was coming but it had gone, you'd have to wait all day. I can't see any other cars or buses or houses or people by the wharf.
Jack	What if a storm came and the dad couldn't get the boat across the channel – where would James go then?
Emma	He might be able to go to those people where he waits each day, but what if they were away?
Emeli	You couldn't take other kids home to play or go to other kids' houses after school. It might be lonely.
Tayla	And you couldn't ring your mum if you forgot your lunch or your gym money – because they couldn't come.
Grayson	It would be good if they had a special machine that could go in the sea and on the road too. One that had wheels that would come down out of the water – then the dad could come any time.
Jack	We could design one!
Teacher	What an interesting idea! You could do this as a language response. You could sketch one and describe to the class how it would work.

Teacher, years 1 to 2

[52] *Island to Island* by M. Bridge

Creating texts

Writing is a creative act, not a set of quantifiable skills to be taught in a predetermined sequence. The teacher's intention is for their students to produce high-quality, accurate writing that achieves its purpose and has an impact on the reader. It's not useful to try to limit a particular kind of writing to a set time in the year. Students need to learn not only that text forms have identifiable features but also that these forms and features can be manipulated to suit various purposes.

As students come to see, with their teacher's help, that writing is like a dialogue between the writer and the developing text, they become increasingly critical readers of their own texts. Just as good readers constantly question the author or the text, good writers, too, ask themselves questions. Effective teachers deliberately promote such questioning through planned activities. By modelling, during shared writing or conferences with students, how writers ask themselves questions, teachers can encourage their students to formulate questions such as the following for themselves: Is my writing making sense? Is the idea worthwhile? Is this expressed in an interesting way? What should I explain further? What should I leave out? Is there another way of writing this? Will the readers be able to imagine what I'm thinking? What am I going to do next?

Anna, a year 4 student, is in conversation with the teacher about her explanation "How does a spider's web form?"

Teacher	I can see that you've worked very hard at this, Anna. You've done really well. What do you think of it?
Anna	I think I'm pleased.
Teacher	Good. You should be. Why are you pleased?
Anna	I planned the order of what happens when a spider makes a web. Then I tried to use lots of different "order" words so that the reader wouldn't get bored.
Teacher	Great. You've used "first", "next", and "then". But remember, we talked about "then" being a boring word if we use it too often. Can you think of any other words you could have used instead?
Anna	Maybe I could have used "after that" or "the next thing"?
Teacher	Maybe. Did you have any problems with your writing?
Anna	I'm not very happy with the ending.
Teacher	Why not?
Anna	Well, it links with my introduction OK, just like you talked about. But I don't think it's as interesting as the introduction.
Teacher	Maybe that's because you wrote just one short sentence as a conclusion? Making your conclusion as interesting as your introduction might be a goal for your next "explanation". What do you think?
Anna	Mmm. Next time I think I'll try to leave the reader with something to think about.

Teachers need to be proactive in motivating students and maintaining their sense of engagement and interest to ensure that the students continue to enjoy writing as they move up through the school. Students need to be engaged in many rich experiences as writers in all three aspects of literacy acquisition, that is, as they encode, create meaning, and become increasingly critically aware and reflective about their own writing.

Students' writing is not confined to a "writing time". It is supported by oral language experiences, by listening to stories, by focused teaching about language, and by talking about their reading and writing.

> A six-year-old boy developed an interest in football. He began asking everyone "Did you see the game?" As the boy became involved with following different teams, he searched a map of the United States to locate the home territories of the football teams – a literacy practice of map reading – and went on to work with a group in constructing informational texts involving detailed investigations and the tabulation of facts. As time went by, the group formed a club to watch games together and began to engage in "surreptitious writing" to organise and amuse themselves.
>
> *For the full account, refer to Dyson, 1999b*

... messages do not come from thin air, nor do they emerge directly from expressive hearts. ... media texts [as well as other overlapping social worlds] provide children with conceptual knowledge, communicative forms and features, and a pool of potential characters, plots, and themes.
Dyson, 1999b, pages 129–130

In a writing conference, the teacher and a student enter into a conversation that focuses on the student's writing. The relationship of those conferring should always be a partnership. With an emergent writer, the talk may focus mainly on establishing the student's intentions, clarifying the topic, or discussing the encoding skills they need to use. As the student meets new challenges and sets new goals, discussion may focus on a specific aspect of the writing process or include questions that encourage elaboration, structural improvements, or the use of new vocabulary to express ideas.

Teachers will find many opportunities during classroom programmes to make links between writing, reading, and oral language. They may draw attention to words or turns of expression both when reading to or with children and in conversations and interactions throughout the day. There's a whole range of written language that can be discussed, including poetic language (for sheer delight in the sounds, rhythm, flow, and power of language) and the language of a transactional text (for its interesting details and its accuracy).

Almost any topic across the curriculum can be used purposefully to stimulate writing. Across the curriculum and throughout the day, teachers can model writing and enable students to practise writing in various forms. For example, teachers and students can add to a wallchart, make jottings in a personal notebook, or write labels for a science experiment.

The writing process and writing strategies

Forming intentions

At this stage, the writer gets an idea, thinks about it in terms of the purpose and audience, and gives it time to grow. As the teacher supports students in forming intentions for their writing, the students will become aware that writing, like reading, is for a purpose.

Depending on the children's age and ability, forming intentions may take some time or may hardly feature at all. For example, beginning writers are usually not so concerned with a target audience and generally work from a model that the teacher provides.

Forming intentions may involve the learner in doing some or all of the following.

What learners do

- decide on the topic or ideas
- decide on the purpose, form, and audience
- make connections with what they already know and with what they have read
- decide on the important ideas
- draw up sections or a rough sequence, using devices such as a graphic organiser when appropriate
- ask questions of themselves and of others to clarify their ideas
- gather information by discussing ideas, locating sources, and selecting information
- create mental images (visualise)
- seek feedback on their ideas and on how to express and organise them
- reflect on their ideas honestly and openly and enjoy a sense of anticipation.

How teachers prompt and support

How do you feel about ...?

What about trying this idea as a poem?

Have you got enough information? How could you find out more?

What would be the best way to put those ideas together?

Who are you writing this for?

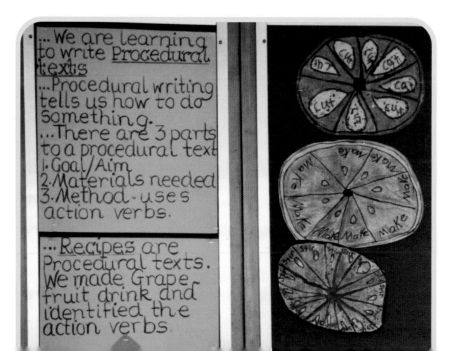

Composing a text

Composing a text involves the writer in translating their thoughts, ideas, intentions, and understandings into a written form. This stage is often described as "getting something down on paper" (even when it involves using a computer). Depending on the focus or shared goal of the activity, the learner may do some or all of the following.

What learners do

- write their ideas down as clearly as possible
- apply their knowledge and awareness of how to use visual and grapho-phonic, semantic, and syntactic information in written texts
- attend to structure and form as well as ideas
- think about the best words to use for the intended audience
- ask themselves questions to clarify their thinking
- seek and act upon feedback from their teacher or peers
- check that they are covering the main points they identified when forming intentions
- check factual accuracy
- shape their text to create links between basic information and further detail
- attend to spelling, grammar, and handwriting (or keyboarding skills).

Beginning writers need lots of modelling and support from the teacher, for example, through shared writing. For them, composing may be painstaking and slow as they:

- develop handwriting skills;
- concentrate on identifying and sequencing the sounds in words.

At the same time, teachers need to help these students to focus on meaning and think about what they are writing.

How teachers prompt and support

How many sounds can you hear in that word? How does it start? What is the end sound? Write down the sounds you can hear.

Where could you go to find out how to write it?

Think about some of those verbs we talked about yesterday.

Which idea do you think should come first?

Do you think you'll need to explain that?

What would make someone want to read your story? How could you start it?

Teachers should provide explicit instruction to ensure that their students develop the ability to form letters and words rapidly and accurately. Beginning writers need to:

- attend closely to the forms and features of letters and clusters of letters;
- attend to visual aspects of print, such as basic punctuation features and spaces between words;
- attend to spelling and handwriting;
- read and reread their work to check what they have done, and think about what they want to do next.

For more fluent writers, words, phrases, and sentences may appear to flow almost automatically. But, as the text develops, the writer will reread it and may find that they need (with the teacher's support) to modify their initial plan. Depending on the focus of the writing task, they may correct details of spelling, punctuation, and grammar. However, at this stage it is important that attention to surface features does not detract from the important focus of giving expression to the writer's intentions.

Revising

Revising generally involves reordering, deleting, and adding text in order to represent an intended meaning more clearly. The writer may search for a more accurate word or expression to capture an idea. At the revising stage, students of all ages reflect critically on what they have written and think about how the audience may respond. At more advanced levels, revision often involves substantial changes to content and structure. Revising may involve the learner in doing some or all of the following.

How teachers prompt and support

Have you told us everything you can about the topic to make it interesting?

What other words could you use here?

Do you think some commas would help here?

How do you want your audience to feel when they read this?

How else could you finish?

I don't understand this part. How could you make it clear?

What learners do

- review how clearly and effectively they have expressed their ideas
- review the purpose or point of view
- review their work critically, for example, for choice of vocabulary and for interest
- ask questions about their intended audience: how will the audience feel when they read this?
- seek and respond to feedback from teacher and peers
- modify the writing as necessary
- attend to surface features.

Students often need encouragement to give careful attention to their writing and to spend time revising it, but it is important that they do so. Learning to revise their writing is essential if they are to become skilled, accurate writers, whether their writing is for personal use or is intended for publishing. The term "editing" is often used for this stage of writing.

Publishing or presenting

Publishing or presenting means making a text available for others to read. This stage may involve completing a number of tasks in preparation for presenting, or it may mean simply sharing a piece with the class by reading it aloud. Publishing or presenting may involve the learner in doing some or all of the following.

What learners do

- make judgments about how to present their writing to the audience
- proof-read their writing, checking for correctness (for example, accurate spelling)
- complete the version to be published or presented
- seek feedback about the published piece from their teacher, peers, and others to inform further learning
- enjoy their own work, share it, and display it.

How teachers prompt and support

This is great writing! What is the most interesting way to set it out?

I think you need to check the spelling again.

Why have you put these words in big letters?

Are some parts more important than others? How could you indicate this?

How will you share your story?

Proof-reading and correcting are part of preparing an accurate text for others to read: they involve spelling, punctuation, grammar, and legibility. Beginning writers need lots of support from the teacher when proof-reading. Often it's best to identify just one or two features for them to check and correct. But all young writers should expect to check their work for accuracy.

By publishing or presenting, writers find out how well they have met their intentions for writing. Warm responses enhance the writer's confidence, and informative feedback from the teacher and their peers gives them guidance for further writing.

Not all pieces of writing are developed to the stage of readiness for sharing with an audience. The purpose of the writing may be very personal, or it may be appropriate that the piece remains a rough draft.

Case study

How Tamyka wrote "My Mum Gives Me a Hug"

The teacher of this year 1 to 2 class worked with her students for three weeks on exploring characterisation in writing. She began by reading and discussing lots of picture books and talking about the concept of "characters" with them. Favourite books included My Dad *by Anthony Browne,* The Kuia and the Spider *by Patricia Grace, and* The Best-loved Bear *by Diana Noonan. Eventually her students started to think about characters as people, animals, or objects.*

Forming intentions

The teacher particularly wanted her students to focus on real people in their writing, especially people who were close to them. She began to promote this focus by getting the students to talk about the mother in the picture book *The Lion in the Meadow*, by Margaret Mahy. They used both visual and text clues in the story to talk about what the mother looked like, what sort of person she was, and how she might have talked. As the students discussed their ideas, the teacher recorded them on the board.

The teacher then asked the students to focus on their own mothers. They had to visualise them in their minds and think about what they were like and what they did. She used the five senses to encourage this thinking – for example, "What does her hair look like?", "How does her voice sound?", and "How does she smell when she hugs you?"

After the discussion, the teacher wrote about her own mother as a model for the students. She particularly reminded them that she was trying to:

- tell her audience what her mother did (main purpose);
- show them how she felt about her mother (second purpose).

In addition, she reminded the students that she was trying to:
- write some new words by getting down all the sounds she could hear;
- use capital letters and full stops well;
- use finger spacing well in her writing.

The students now understood what they needed to do. Tamyka, the writer of this text, had a clear purpose for writing: to tell what her mother did and show how she felt about her. She also knew that her teacher expected her to try some new words in her writing and to use capital letters, full stops, and finger spacing well.

She was excited about writing because she had now clearly visualised all the relevant things about her mother and knew what she wanted to say. Her teacher had helped her visualise these images through conversation:

Teacher	I see your mum drop you off at school sometimes. What does she do when she says goodbye?
Tamyka	She gives me a hug.
Teacher	What a lovely mum. I like it when my mum hugs me.

Composing the text

Tamyka drafted her piece of writing. To begin with, she drew a picture of her mum. This helped her to focus on her main message: "My mum always gives me a hug when she drops me off at school."

As Tamyka wrote, she used her prior knowledge of sound, letter, word, and sentence formation. In particular, she:

- articulated her sentence to the teacher before she began to write;
- made connections with key content words that were modelled by the teacher ("mum");
- used her knowledge of high-frequency words well ("my", "me", "she", "at");
- used her "sounding-out" skills in trying out new words ("owas", "gve", "hag", "scol");
- used a capital letter, a full stop, and a space between the lines.

Revising the text

The teacher helped Tamyka to revise her story. While roving, she realised that Tamyka could add more to her story because she had not yet met the second purpose for writing ("Show how you feel about your mother"). So she asked Tamyka focused questions that led her to add a second sentence.

Teacher	How do you feel when your mum hugs you?
Tamyka	It feels warm. She goes like this (demonstrates by hugging herself).
Teacher	Her arms wrap around you and make you feel warm. Can you write that?

Tamyka not only used the teacher's modelled sentence structure and vocabulary to help her; she also used her own knowledge of key content and high-frequency words ("and", "with", "two") and her sounding-out skills ("ams", "wom", "hods").

She read her story again and was pleased because she knew that she had now met the purposes for writing. This also gave her the confidence to feel that her audience – the teacher and the other students – would enjoy her writing and respond positively to it.

Publishing and presenting the writing

Tamyka wanted to present her writing in two ways.

- She wanted her teacher to read and respond to the final version. Her teacher did this and affirmed not only the lovely feelings in the story but also Tamyka's ability to meet the success criteria. The teacher also focused on Tamyka's still developing familiarity with the sounds "dr" and "l" in writing.
- Tamyka wanted to read it aloud to her class and get an oral response from her classmates. She did this, and they loved it!

Technical skills for writing

Spelling

Writers need to develop the ability to use conventional spelling in order to write clearly, fluently, and accurately. This involves moving through a number of stages.[53] To become a proficient speller, a writer has to develop various kinds of knowledge, strategies for spelling unknown words, and awareness of how to use their knowledge and strategies.

Learning to spell is a developmental process; it goes hand in hand with learning to write. Young learners normally begin with scribbles. Then, as they come to understand that writers use letters to write down the words used in spoken language, they may write strings of letters so that their writing contains "words". As they develop further knowledge of how the alphabet is used, they learn that letters are used to write down the sounds that make up words and begin to use letter-sound correspondences in their writing. Beginning spellers usually learn to write the beginning or end sounds of words, which are often consonants, before they can isolate and write medial sounds, which are usually vowels (see Relating parts of words to sounds, on page 36). Reading and writing experiences provide young learners with knowledge about spelling patterns (orthography) and about the rules and conventions that apply to words (morphology). They then use this knowledge in further learning.

Students are exposed to correct spellings through reading a wide range of texts. However, not all students develop the detailed knowledge that they need simply through exposure to print. Students need to be taught explicitly how to use the common orthographic and morphological structures of written English for spelling (encoding) words in English.

Developing spelling knowledge

The teacher needs to support students to enable them to:

- use their phonemic awareness;
- use their knowledge of letter-sound relationships;
- develop a knowledge of orthographic patterns;
- develop a knowledge of the morphological structure of written English.

Students use their phonemic awareness in spelling to break words into phonemes. The child who is able to write every sound in an unknown word is demonstrating phonemic segmentation skills. For example, a child might spell "jump" (with four sounds) g, a, m, p (for the four sounds).

Students use their knowledge of letter-sound relationships, that is, of phonics, to write the letters for the sounds they have identified.

---

[53] Refer to pages 64–70 of *Dancing with the Pen* for information about these stages.

Students need a knowledge of orthographic patterns – that is, of the spelling patterns that represent sounds in words. The teacher can help the students to develop this knowledge by encouraging them to make analogies to known words that sound the same or look the same. Beginning spellers need to be exposed to ways of writing all sounds (not just those that are commonly associated with the alphabet letters) since they will be trying to write words such as **look**, **out**, **now**, h**ou**se, t**oy**, b**oo**t, tr**ai**n, and tr**ee**.

> "I tuk my nyou t_ to the prk akros the rod from my hows."
>
> "I took my new toy to the park across the road from my house."
>
> The child does not know how to write the"oy" and "ar" sounds. They have used what they know from "put" to write "took" and from "you" to write "new". Phonetically and orthographically, this is an excellent attempt, but it also tells the teacher that the child needs to learn that "ar" and "oy" are separate sounds that have particular ways of being written in words.

Students need a knowledge of the morphological structure of written English, that is, of the rules and conventions that underlie conventional spelling patterns. Teachers need to show their students how to transfer knowledge about conventions of print from one word that they have learned to spell by sight to other words that have a similar sound or use the same convention.

> A child has learned to spell "played" and "jumped" using the "ed" ending. Although the "ed" ending sounds different in these two words ("play**d**", "jump**t**"), the child has worked out that the "ed" ending is added to words that mean something has already happened even though the words might sound different at the end ("t", "d", and "id" in "end**id**"). When they meet a new word that describes something they did yesterday, one that they do not recognise as a sight word, they can use the correct convention to spell the word ending ("Yesterday I hopp**ed** all the way down the path").

Through engaging learners with texts, teachers can model and explain the use of such conventions as apostrophes in contractions, adding "s" for a plural, and putting two "p's" in stopping (doing the same when they want to write "hopping" or "shopping"). Students who apply this knowledge demonstrate a developing awareness of morphological structure.

Helping students to move towards accurate spelling

Teachers need to support their students in moving from producing strings of letters to spelling approximations and then to accurate conventional spelling. They can do so in the following ways.

- *Model how to break the word the student wants to use into individual sounds.*

- *Prompt the student to relate the sounds in the word to letters or letter patterns they already know.* The teacher can help them to draw analogies to words they know that sound the same and have the same spelling patterns, for example, by saying "What is a word you know that has the same sound as …?"

- *Give feedback acknowledging the parts of the word that are correct and accepting and expanding on approximations that make sense and show that the student is acquiring spelling knowledge and strategies.* For example, a student may use the correct number of syllables or make correct letter-sound connections. When a student spells "kat" for "cat", every sound in the word is correct, even though the spelling pattern used is not the accepted one.

- *Lead students towards self-correction by giving them appropriate feedback that informs them about accuracies and inaccuracies in the way they have written a word.* For example, the teacher can say, "You've used correct letters for all the sounds in 'cat' but, in this word, we use the letter 'c' to write the 'k' sound."

- *Model correct spelling by comparing unknown words with similar known words (and explaining the different patterns).* For example, when a student spells "awful" as "orful", the teacher can say, "You know how to spell 'saw' in 'I saw a bird'; how do you write the 'or' sound in 'saw'?" The teacher can then explain that the "or" sound in "awful" uses the same pattern – which is also used in "lawn" and "yawn" and "awesome".

- *Use questions and prompts, during shared and guided reading and in writing activities, to reinforce their students' knowledge of spelling patterns and conventions.* For example, the teacher can ask, "Who can find me a word that has a 'ch' sound in it? What letters are used for writing the 'ch' sound in 'chicken'?"

- *Analyse each student's spelling errors to identify specific knowledge or strategies that the student may need more help to master, and provide specific instruction to meet these needs.*

- *Ensure that each student continues to develop a bank of words that they can spell automatically.*

Models of accurately spelled words can be recorded in individual spelling notebooks (personal dictionaries). New words should be added regularly for students to refer to and revise, as appropriate to their stage of spelling development. The student should understand the meanings of the words they are learning to spell, which should arise from their reading and writing experiences. Words from their personal writing have meaning for students and so are relevant for their spelling notebooks.

Most teachers make a range of high-frequency words readily accessible, for example, on a wallchart or on large cards. A class dictionary, in alphabetical order, is a valuable resource for the group to use during shared writing and for students to refer to when writing independently. Entries can be made after talking through the students' approximations, and the dictionary should be constantly used and expanded.

... knowing forty to fifty words will cover almost all the letters, many high-frequency words, many common-letter clusters, and some orthographic or spelling patterns useful for getting to other words ... The words can be constructed or remembered, or taken apart and used in analogies.

Clay, 1998, page 149

Approximations in spelling

An approximation is a word that a child writes using spelling that is not completely correct but is as close as they can manage to the word they want to spell. It is generally good practice to suggest that children "have a go" at writing a word by themselves before seeking help. This will encourage them to use the knowledge, awareness, and strategies that they have (see page 26).

Teachers should regularly model ways of attending to spelling. Because beginning spellers do not know how to spell many words, they need to use the sounds in unknown words to guide their spelling attempts. The ability to discriminate between and segment sounds in words is a critical skill and is based on phonemic awareness (see page 32). Teachers can model how to break words into sounds and then write these sounds using known letters and letter patterns. When there are two or more possibilities for spelling one sound, teachers should demonstrate or explain that for this word, this particular pattern is used to write the sounds. For example, when writing the word "they", many students who can spell "play" and "day" will write it "thay". The teacher should model the correct spelling – "they" – and explain that, in this word, the long "a" sound is written "ey", not "ay".

... the value of encouraging and allowing young children to invent their spelling has been strongly supported by well-conducted studies .... When children attempt to represent their speech with letters, they are applying phonics in a truly authentic context.

Templeton and Morris, 1999, page 108

As students gain more knowledge of spelling, they can be shown how to use dictionaries, word lists, and electronic spellcheckers to ensure that conventionally correct spellings are resulting from their decisions.

Students need to become aware that they should spell the words they use in their writing correctly. However, spelling must also be kept in context.[54] The writer's main aim is to convey meaning. Too much concentration on accurate spelling, especially during draft writing, can reduce the focus on conveying a meaningful message and may make students tentative and unadventurous in their writing.

---

[54] Note too that spelling can vary for different purposes (such as text messaging and advertising) and audiences (such as a British audience or an American audience).

Analysing the nature of spelling attempts in children's writing will show the teacher the skills and knowledge the child has and the gaps they need to fill.

- If a child is not writing all the sounds in a word, the teacher needs to consider whether this is because they cannot hear them all (due to hearing issues or lack of phonemic segmentation skills) or whether they do not yet know a letter or letter pattern for writing the sound.

- If a child can write all the sounds with an appropriate but incorrect letter or letter pattern, the teacher knows that they are ready to learn more about the possible spelling patterns for different sounds.

- If a child can use a spelling convention for one word (they can spell "can't" using an apostrophe correctly) but cannot apply it to other words (they are not able to spell "won't" or "didn't"), the teacher knows that they have learned "can't" by sight and need to be taught the principle of how contractions work and to practise applying the convention.

Everything a teacher needs to know about children's developing spelling knowledge is displayed in their writing. The best starting point is to look for what they are able to do when they write unknown words.

Handwriting

Students' handwriting develops in the course of their experiences of writing. Almost every child enjoys the physical act of drawing, but developing the precision required to form letters is a challenge for many.[55]

Initially, the teacher needs to accept some irregularities, especially where an undue emphasis on letter forms could interrupt a young writer's flow of thought. However, students need explicit instruction in letter formation so that they do not develop habits that prevent them from writing fluently and legibly. Teachers can note the aspects that need working on and provide opportunities for their students to practise them, for example, by having practice cards available in the writing corner.

Writing using computers

Studies show the power of small group work at the computer to generate thinking and discussion, and the advantages of using a word processor for the joint construction of text.

Downes and Fatouros, 1995, page 7

Evidence of the value of using a keyboard and computer screen for writing is more consistent than for other uses of computers in a literacy programme. Studies emphasise that small-group, collaborative work makes the best use of the opportunities offered by electronic communications technology.[56]

The teacher can provide focused support when working with a group of students using computers for writing. The computer supports students' writing development because it enables them to revise a text quickly and easily without the manual labour of rewriting. This enables them to focus more on their ideas and on the process they are using, which helps them to develop metacognitive understandings about the process of constructing meaning through writing.

---

[55] The basic script recommended for schools and suggestions for teaching it effectively are presented in the Department of Education handbook *Teaching Handwriting*.

[56] Downes and Fatouros (1995) cite some sources of evidence.

Constructing a text together, as pairs or in a group, enhances the co-operative atmosphere of the classroom as a community of learners (see also the sections on pages 104–108 on shared and guided writing). It's especially helpful to children whose backgrounds emphasise the value of working with others. Using email can provide a context for teaching writing for a range of audiences and purposes. Expecting feedback from correspondents provides added motivation for writers.

Ongoing instruction to engage learners with texts

Students who have gained proficiency and independence in reading and creating texts need ongoing support and motivation and new challenges in text activities. Sometimes teachers may assume that direct instruction in reading and writing is no longer needed. However, new emphases in teacher instruction become important as students increasingly encounter texts in subject areas with new demands in terms of specialist vocabulary, presentation of content, and concepts. Approaches like reading to students, shared reading and writing, and guided reading and writing remain relevant throughout the school years. The teacher's support and guidance are also still needed in text selection and in encouraging silent reading, recreational reading, and independent writing.

Further reading

For full reference details of the resources listed here, refer to pages 189–194.

Guidance on engaging learners with texts to improve literacy achievement is contained in such texts as:

Anderson, K. (2001). *Motivating the Reluctant Writer.*

Block, C. C. and Pressley, M., eds (2002). *Comprehension Instruction: Research-based Best Practices.*

Braunger, J. and Lewis, J. (1998). *Building a Knowledge Base in Reading.*

Hood, H. (1997). *Left to Write Too.*

Ministry of Education (1992). *Dancing with the Pen.*

Ministry of Education (1996b). *The Learner as a Reader: Developing Reading Programmes.*

Ministry of Education (1997b). *Reading and Beyond: Discovering Language through Ready to Read.*

Ministry of Education (2001b). *Ready to Read Teacher Support Material: Emergent Level.*

Ministry of Education (2002b). *Ready to Read Teacher Support Material: Early Levels.*

Mooney, M. (2001). *Text Forms and Features: A Resource for Intentional Teaching.*

Pressley, M. (2002c). *Reading Instruction That Works: The Case for Balanced Teaching.*

Smith, J. and Elley, W. (1997a). *How Children Learn to Read.*

Smith, J. and Elley, W. (1997b). *How Children Learn to Write.*

Sweet, A. P. and Snow, C. E. (2003). *Rethinking Reading Comprehension.*

Thompson, L. M. (2002). *Guided Reading: Years 1–4.*

Studies and commentary on effectively engaging learners with texts to meet diverse needs include:

Au, K. H. (2002). "Multicultural Factors and the Effective Instruction of Students of Diverse Backgrounds".

Dyson, A. H. (1997). *Writing Superheroes: Contemporary Childhood, Popular Culture, and Classroom Literacy.*

Dyson, A. H. (1999a). "Transforming Transfer: Unruly Children, Contrary Texts and the Persistence of the Pedagogical Order".

Dyson, A. H. (1999b). "Writing (Dallas) Cowboys: A Dialogic Perspective on the 'What Did I Write?' Question".

McNaughton, S. (2002). *Meeting of Minds.*

Ministry of Education (1999b). *Non-English-Speaking-Background Students: A Handbook for Schools.*

Phillips, G., McNaughton, S., and MacDonald, S. (2000). *Picking up the Pace: Effective Literacy Interventions for Accelerated Progress over the Transition into Decile 1 Schools.*

Turoa, L., Wolfgramm, E., Tanielu, L., and McNaughton, S. (2002). *Pathways over the Transition to Schools: Studies in Family Literacy Practices and Effective Classroom Contexts for Māori and Pasifika Children.*

Chapter 6:

Expectations

Introduction

Expectations are the ideas that teachers, children, parents, and communities have about children as learners – about their knowledge and expertise, their progress, and their achievement.

This chapter focuses on teachers' expectations, which are shaped by:

• their beliefs and values;

• their professional and theoretical knowledge.

Teachers' expectations can be defined as inferences about their students' future behaviour or achievement based on the teachers' current knowledge of these students. The expectations that teachers have for their students influence various aspects of their practice, including:

• goal setting and assessment;

• the nature of their interactions with their students;

• the amount of interaction between teacher and students;

• their selection and use of instructional strategies;

• the text-based experiences that they plan for the students.

Students, too, have expectations about their learning and their progress. At school entry, children typically have high expectations for themselves – they expect to learn about many things. Their expectations for their own literacy learning develop from hearing and seeing others in the family and community reading and writing; these experiences are part of their early socialisation into literacy. They expect that they will enjoy learning and that the teacher will want to know about them and will expect them to succeed. Effective teachers know this and build on it by engaging their students in focused and appropriate activities.

Parents also have expectations. They expect their child to be taught, to learn, and to make progress. They expect the teacher to have expertise and commitment. Chapter 7 discusses the importance of the teacher's role in providing parents with information to help them clarify their expectations for their children's learning and in developing shared goals with them.

Teachers will be aware that at a national level, society has expectations about the literacy learning and achievement of students in New Zealand schools. These expectations are set out in the New Zealand Curriculum.

Teachers' expectations for their students should be high but appropriate and should also be:

• informed by their professional knowledge and based on evidence;

• clearly expressed;

- shared with all partners in the student's learning;
- informed by feedback from all partners in the student's learning;
- reflected upon and reviewed in the light of evidence about their effects.

The impact of expectations on achievement

Many studies have demonstrated the relationship between teachers' expectations and outcomes for students.[57] These studies provide evidence that teachers form beliefs about the potential of different students and groups of students to achieve and that these beliefs are translated into goals that reflect the teachers' expectations for those students. Teachers' expectations shape their decisions about tasks, programmes, and instruction. In many cases, the outcome is that students perceived as high achievers are set more demanding tasks, while those expected to be low achievers are set tasks requiring lower level skills.

Teachers' expectations affect their ability to motivate and engage their students, which, in turn, affects student outcomes (see page 22).

Teachers' expectations should be informed by data and based on evidence. They should also be informed by a knowledge of the patterns of children's progress in literacy learning (see pages 70-74) and by other sources of information. Teachers' knowledge about literacy learning influences their expectations, which is why this book has a focus on knowledge about how children become literate.

Expectations and low-achievement patterns

The impact of expectations is especially significant for students from diverse cultural and linguistic backgrounds. The expectations held by the students themselves, their parents and extended families, the school staff, and especially their teachers have a huge impact. Low or negative expectations affect not only a student's progress and achievements but also their self-image and sense of identity.

The challenge for many teachers is to move away from associating "difference" with deficit. Teachers can limit their students' potential by limiting their expectations for what the students can achieve.

The research evidence has shown a common pattern, in New Zealand schools, of teachers and other staff having lower expectations for certain identified groups of students, particularly Māori and Pasifika students in low-decile schools and NESB students.

Effective teachers have expectations that children can achieve academic progress and believe that they can be effective in helping to do this. For example, in literacy, they believe that their children can attain independence in reading and writing, and they continually look for opportunities to move them up a gradient of difficulty, with appropriate interactive support.

Keith, 2002, page 12, summarising Phillips, McNaughton, and MacDonald, 2000

---

[57] Studies that provide this evidence are listed at the end of this chapter.

Studies in such schools and classrooms have revealed that teachers have often:

- underestimated how much these students knew and could do at school entry;
- underestimated the rate at which these students could be expected to progress;
- assumed that the parents of these children lacked commitment and did not have the level of interest, or the ability, to contribute to their child's education (for example, by hearing their child read each evening);
- assumed that these students needed to be at school for some time before they were "ready" for formal instruction.

This example shows how a school's review of achievement data led to a shift in teachers' expectations based on the evidence that they gathered.

A school review of the achievement of year 3 students in a large urban school showed that 50 percent of them were achieving at levels one-and-a-half to two years below national norms. This two-year delay in achievement continued throughout the children's primary schooling. The teachers attributed the results at year 3 to the children's low skills at school entry and the consequent amount of time they had to spend teaching these early skills. Staff could cite many examples of inadequate and inappropriate early skills, for example, children eating crayons because they could not distinguish them from food and were unaware that they were a writing tool.

The teachers decided to focus on improving these skills. They developed a list of twenty-five skills that they believed were critical for children to master before the teachers could begin "school-level" instruction. These skills were divided into five groups, comprising early reading (for example, realise that print and pictures carry a message), writing (for example, tell others what to write), language (for example, follow an instruction), social (for example, work independently for a short time), and motor skills (for example, use a pair of scissors). New entrant teachers surveyed the next forty new entrant children on their mastery of these skills.

The deputy principal collated the individual results. The teachers who had completed the assessments were asked to estimate the aggregated results. All but one predicted that the children had mastered, on average, 30 to 40 percent of the skills on the list. The remaining teacher predicted a much higher level – 70 to 80 percent – of skill acquisition. The aggregated results revealed a picture very different from what most of the teachers had expected. The average percentage of skills mastered was in fact 74 percent. Only seven children scored less than 50 percent, with fifteen children scoring above 90 percent. Given that the checklist items were the teachers' definition of what was required for school learning, the deputy principal's conclusions were not surprising: "We must conclude from this survey that the five-year-olds entering the school bring with them a very sound foundation for learning." Closer analysis of reading achievement scores revealed that the one teacher who accurately estimated higher skill levels achieved the best reading outcomes for the children.

Raising teachers' expectations can be a critical factor in breaking the pattern of low achievement – in terms of both the learning that students are capable of and the pace at which they are able to progress.[58] Teachers who succeed in improving outcomes for students from diverse cultural and linguistic backgrounds may differ from one another in their styles of teaching and may run different kinds of programmes. What they have in common is a set of beliefs: at heart, they believe firmly that all students can learn and be successful academically in the school setting.[59]

Implications for teachers

Part of teachers' professionalism is being prepared to shift their practice when they see evidence that this can improve outcomes for their students. For teachers, being professional means raising their awareness in the face of evidence, being prepared to confront their own beliefs and assumptions, and being willing to accept that data may need to be explained in terms of what the teacher believes and does. It means accepting that they cannot continue to attribute disparities in achievement to out-of-school factors, such as family circumstances or low income.

Teachers need to be clear about their expectations for their students, and they need to be able to articulate them. Teachers' expectations should be discussed both at syndicate level and school-wide. Through a dynamic process involving professional dialogue, a school can effectively review and refine its expectations for its students. These expectations may be presented as generally agreed indicators, like those set out on pages 71–74.

When all partners with an interest in a student's learning share data to inform each others' expectations, the outcomes for students are likely to be positive. (See chapter 7.)

Teachers who know about, value, and draw upon the diverse experiences and the expertise that their students bring to school are likely to hold higher expectations for their students and to be more effective in their practice.[60]

The teacher's expectations need to be appropriate in terms of the multiple pathways that children take in their learning. Informed and appropriate expectations are particularly important for students with special needs, NESB students, those making rapid progress, and those experiencing difficulties. The teacher may need specialist advice or support in order to provide effectively for their students' range of learning needs.

---

[58] Refer to Phillips, McNaughton, and MacDonald (2000).

[59] Refer to Ladson-Billings (1994).

[60] Refer to Ministry of Education (2003a).

Teachers need to reflect on their expectations and review them (as they do with all the dimensions of teaching practice). Reflections about the reasons for students' different rates of progress are most likely to lead to improved outcomes when the reflections are underpinned by a belief that all students can succeed.

Professional dialogue is a powerful tool. Studies have shown that teachers who form a learning community in the school are willing to gather and confront evidence about their teaching and learning and to explore and challenge their practices and beliefs collegially. They are prepared to analyse the effectiveness of their own practice. As a result of such analysis, teachers have shifted their practice; as a direct result of the shift in practice, students have made visible progress – and as a result of seeing this progress, teachers have shifted their beliefs.

Shifts in teachers' practice that are associated with higher expectations for students and with improved student achievement are characterised by:

- intensified, explicit instruction;
- goal setting;
- rich experiences with texts;
- monitoring of students' progress;
- informative feedback to students.

These features of good practice benefit all students, but they are particularly effective when used with those students for whom expectations have traditionally been low. Effective classroom practice in relation to these students reflects the following beliefs and expectations:

- All students have expertise and can succeed.
- Elements of home literacy practices can usefully be incorporated into classroom activities.
- Literacy instruction should cover all three aspects of literacy learning – not only learning the code and making meaning but also thinking critically and engaging with texts at deeper levels.
- Focused instruction should begin at school entry.

I used to think that when my new entrant children first arrived, they only needed to be looked after – that I had to wait until they had settled in and seemed "ready" to learn. As long as they were busy and happy and had made a friend, I was satisfied, and underneath I know I had the feeling that they didn't know much. Now they're not long in the door before we're into focused learning. I use the information from enrolment and from my own observations of them on their first day or two to decide how to take their learning on from where they are. They're ready, all right, and they know a lot.

Finally, teachers need to consider their expectations in terms of routines and management and of how they communicate with all learners in the course of the school day. These expectations, too, are part of a teacher's belief system and influence their practice. They may relate to how different students will participate in classroom literacy activities and to certain students' potential for maintaining focus, working independently, making choices, or taking responsibility for classroom tasks. Such expectations can be conveyed in subtle ways, many of which are non-verbal. Children internalise these messages and reflect them in their own attitudes and actions.

Further reading

For full reference details of the resources listed here, refer to pages 189–194.

Research evidence about the impact of expectations on student achievement is summarised in:

Ministry of Education (2003a). *Quality Teaching for Diverse Students in Schooling: Best Evidence Synthesis.*

Further studies and commentary about expectations and student achievement (particularly in relation to low-achievement patterns) include:

Bishop, R. and Glynn, T. (1999). *Culture Counts: Changing Power Relations in Education.*

Bishop, R. and Glynn, T. (2000). "Kaupapa Māori Messages for the Mainstream".

Darling-Hammond, L. (1997). *The Right to Learn: A Blueprint for Creating Schools That Work.*

Delpit, L. (1995). *Other People's Children: Cultural Conflict in the Classroom.*

Keith, M. (2002). *Picking up the Pace: A Summary.*

Ladson-Billings, G. (1994). *The Dream Keepers: Successful Teachers of African American Children.*

McNaughton, S. (2002). *Meeting of Minds.*

Phillips, G., McNaughton, S., and MacDonald, S. (2000). *Picking up the Pace: Effective Literacy Interventions for Accelerated Progress over the Transition into Decile 1 Schools.*

Timperley, H. S. and Robinson, V. M. J. (2001). *Achieving School Improvement through Challenging and Changing Teachers' Schema.*

Timperley, H. S., Robinson, V. M. J., and Bullard, T. (1999). *Strengthening Education in Māngere and Ōtara Evaluation: First Evaluation Report.*

Turoa, L., Wolfgramm, E., Tanielu, L., and McNaughton, S. (2002). *Pathways over the Transition to Schools: Studies in Family Literacy Practices and Effective Classroom Contexts for Māori and Pasifika Children.*

Chapter 7:

Partnerships

Introduction

Partnerships are collaborative relationships that contribute to and support students' learning. They are active, planned, and dynamic. Effective partners complement and respect one another and value each other's contributions. Together they form a network of significant people with a common interest in a child's learning. Each partner has a particular role in the relationship, takes responsibility for that role, and is accountable to the other partners.

Teachers need to work in close partnership with all who have a stake in the student's learning. Quality partnerships are built on shared understandings and shared goals for the student's literacy development. Like all relationships, they require commitment, trust, and empathy. Actively promoting such relationships with partners in students' literacy development is part of effective practice for all classroom teachers. Like all the dimensions of effective practice in this book, partnerships can be described as effective only if they demonstrably contribute to improved outcomes for students.

In effective partnerships, all partners have:

- shared expectations;
- shared knowledge about the learner;
- shared knowledge about literacy teaching and learning;
- shared knowledge and valuing of the learner's background of experience.

Partners in literacy learning support one another and celebrate the learners' achievements together.

Home-school partnerships

Partnerships between homes and schools are most likely to be effective when they are based on shared expectations – that is, when all partners believe that the student will succeed as a learner. These expectations need to be appropriate and informed so that shared goals can be developed. Teachers have a role in clarifying the expectations that they have for their students' learning and communicating these to families (see chapter 6).

Schools and teachers often underestimate the level of parents' commitment to – even eagerness about – their child's education. Parents, on their part, may assume that the school is not interested in the literacy activities of the home or that they themselves cannot contribute to their child's literacy learning. Teachers need to be proactive in order to counter any perceptions that only in-school learning counts.

Sharing knowledge about the learner (see chapter 3) contributes to strong partnerships. When both partners share their knowledge:

- the teacher can explain the child's level of achievement, in detail, to parents, for example, through discussing samples of the child's work;
- the parents or caregivers can describe their child's achievements;
- both partners know about and value the learner's background of experience because the family shares information about home and community literacy practices, including the knowledge, expertise, and activities involved;
- the teacher uses the knowledge of these practices in their planning;
- the parents or caregivers regularly meet to set and discuss literacy goals with their children and their children's teachers;
- the child, the teacher, and the parents or caregivers regularly share feedback about the child's progress towards these goals;
- the teacher is aware of any changing circumstances in a child's family life that may affect their performance;
- the parents, the teacher, and the child can celebrate the child's achievements together.

Home-school partnerships are most effective when they are based on shared knowledge about literacy teaching and learning, that is, when:

- teachers help parents to become familiar with the classroom literacy practices and parents explain home literacy practices and events to teachers;
- teachers help parents and caregivers to develop understandings about important aspects of literacy learning, such as reading and writing with children and having conversations with them;
- teachers explain and model strategies to parents and caregivers to help them support their child's progress in literacy learning;
- the school ensures that appropriate resources in English and in their home languages are available to help families support their children's literacy learning.

… teachers are often inclined to have assumptions and expectations about parental interest and support that are socially or ethnoculturally biased. Studies over many years have pointed to educators' misjudgements about parental involvement – for example, misconstruing failure to attend meetings as failure to support their children or the school.

Hargreaves, 2000, page 172

... all families in the school community will understand that they are the school community. All families will be included and involved in school activities and will feel completely comfortable in their school.

Ministry of Education, 2003c, page 6

Teachers may use a variety of community settings and resources, as appropriate, when sharing information and discussing children's learning needs with families, for example, by arranging to meet families on a marae or in a community church hall. Many teachers have found that family and community members feel more at ease in such circumstances and are more likely to enter into a balanced partnership than when schools communicate through traditional means, such as newsletters or parent-teacher interviews at the school.

When the children's teachers and their families take advantage of informal face-to-face encounters to show a warm personal interest in each other and in building up a relationship, the development of an effective home-school partnership is facilitated.

The impact of home-school partnerships on students' learning

A significant relationship exists between parents' active involvement in their child's learning and the child's achievement. There is evidence of strong and sustained improvement in children's achievement when the home-school partnership:

- has the child's learning as its focus (although children may gain some benefit through other forms of parental involvement, for example, when parents take part in voluntary work for the school);
- is supported by school-wide policies and practices, for example, when the school has effective processes for making parents feel welcome and sharing information with them.

Children's literacy achievement improves when their parents participate in structured programmes that build parents' understanding of literacy learning and provide simple strategies that they can use to help their children learn.

There is also evidence that home-school partnerships may bring indirect benefits. For example, successful efforts to build home-school links have resulted in family members becoming willing to come into the school and in parents meeting each other to share experiences and ideas.

Studies show that students benefit when their teachers plan for some continuity between school and home literacy practices, particularly where there is significant divergence between them. Positive outcomes occur when:

- teachers build on the cultural processes and practices of students' homes;
- families and communities become familiar with the literacy practices of the classroom and support these in their home activities.

International studies have also identified the barriers to productive partnerships, especially partnerships with low-income families and families from minority groups.[61] Where the ethnic or linguistic background of the student's family differs from that of the dominant school culture, a lack of dialogue between home and school can result in both parties assuming that the other lacks commitment to the students' learning.

[61] For example, refer to Ramey and Ramey (1998), Wolfgramm, McNaughton, and Afeaki (1997), Glynn, Berryman, and Glynn (2000), and Snow, Burns, and Griffin (1998).

The parents can then feel alienated from the school, and this has a negative effect on their children's learning.

We are a large decile 2 urban school. Some 60 percent of our students are of Pasifika heritage, 20 percent are Māori, 10 percent are Pākehā, and other ethnic groups make up the remainder. During a literacy review, the staff agreed that a primary goal for literacy development would be to form dynamic partnerships with the parents or caregivers in our learning community. The aim was to foster parent support in raising student achievement in literacy.

As a first step, we collected and analysed data, which confirmed that the proportion of NESB students in the school population was high, in fact, just over a third. The data on forthcoming enrolments suggested a similar proportion.

The staff included those who used two languages. This was valuable in establishing and maintaining relationships because many parents and caregivers were more comfortable discussing their children's needs in the family's first language.

To enable the staff to build their knowledge of the students' home backgrounds, we produced newsletters and organised events – meetings, open days at the school, school sports, and school performances. The networking enabled the community and staff to learn from each other.

Lead teachers were established within the school, and bilingual lead parents were identified within the community. These parents and teachers worked as a team at parent meetings to deliver key messages and to model ways to support the students' literacy learning. For these meetings, childcare was arranged and the parents "turned up in all sorts of weather". Parents found it valuable to share with each other, and some parents met others from their own ethnic group for the first time.

As the relationships developed, the parents felt less threatened, and they increasingly appreciated the value both of their role and of their own language in developing their children's learning. A key success factor in the partnership process was identifying the lead people in the community and providing them with knowledge about literacy learning. Their support for the other parents and caregivers was invaluable.

We began to notice an increase in the students' self-esteem, sense of identity, and confidence as learners. To our delight, they are reading more, both in English and in their home language. The parents and caregivers have also become more confident in supporting their children, which has had a significant impact on the children's performance and attitude in all areas – academic, social, and sporting.

We analysed our data and found noticeable improvements in the students' literacy achievement over the year. We had exceeded our own goals and have now had to raise them.

In-school partnerships

The teacher has a responsibility for networking with others in the school who are involved in their students' learning. These people include teacher aides, classroom volunteer helpers, the librarian, those involved in interventions, and specialist support staff or service providers. The aim is to ensure consistency, collaboration, and appropriateness in how all partners:

- establish expectations for the student's progress;
- gather and share information about the student's progress;
- analyse and interpret this information;
- seek and give feedback about the student's progress and learning needs;
- make decisions when specific action is called for, including decisions about interventions and about seeking specialist advice or support.

Children's peers are among the significant people in their lives and influence their values, attitudes, and behaviours. The teacher has a role to play in fostering positive and healthy relationships among the students in the classroom. In a well-planned literacy programme, peer groups, buddies, or peer tutors can all be part of the network of partners who contribute to the children's literacy development.

Partnerships between children of the same cultural or linguistic background can support cultural values and home languages; this support can be particularly valuable for learning. The tuakana-teina relationship, an integral part of traditional Māori society, provides a great model for buddy systems (an older or more expert "brother", "sister", or "cousin" supports and guides a younger or less expert one).

Partnerships for interventions

A literacy intervention occurs when a student receives literacy instruction that is additional to the classroom programme, for example, when a student attends reading recovery sessions or when an NESB student is supported by a trained ESOL (English for Speakers of Other Languages) teacher. It is very important to have effective networking processes in place when decisions about beginning or ending interventions are being made. Such processes are also important during the interventions.

Interventions have an impact on the student's self-esteem as well as on their pathway of progress, so the period of the actual intervention and the period following it are both times of potential risk for the student and their learning.

Teachers need to know about the learning activities in the intervention and to build on these in the classroom programme during and after the intervention. Similarly, those responsible for the intervention need to work in with the classroom teacher.

Partnerships for transitions

Effective partnerships are very important during times of transition. A transition involves a child moving between two teaching and learning contexts. The challenge for the classroom teacher lies in providing the right kind and amount of support for students during their change of learning environment. To provide such support, it's necessary to have processes in place for sharing information about the student and their learning. The teacher's role in managing transitions includes taking responsibility for a student's progress even when the student is in the class (or the intervention) for only a short time.

A transition may involve the student moving:

• from home to school;

• from early childhood centre to school;

• within the school (particularly from one class to another);

• between schools;

• from one language setting to another;

• between intervention programme and classroom programme;

• to a school in a new country.

Refugee students and their teachers may find the transition to a New Zealand school especially challenging.

The biggest challenge for teachers in managing transitions is ensuring continuity in children's learning. Part of this challenge is working with the other partners in the children's learning: better connections among those involved mean better opportunities for learning. When students move from one class to another, it is particularly important that information about their learning and progress is passed on and used. At these times, up-to-date assessment data and accurate analysis of the data are especially useful for informing teachers' decisions about students' learning.

This is an example of how a school has developed partnerships to facilitate children's transition to school.

Our school draws from a community of diverse backgrounds. To enhance children's transition to school, we have developed ways of working in partnership with the community because we recognise the crucial nature of this time for children and their learning. Our aim is to build shared knowledge and expectations for all partners: the child, their parents, their teachers, and early childhood centre staff.

Each term, reciprocal visits are made between the school and the early childhood centres from which the school draws. These visits are mutually valuable, enabling all partners to build up knowledge about the children and their learning programmes.

We keep a register of pre-schoolers, updating it regularly because of the degree of transience in the community. Then, four weeks before each child is expected to arrive at school, we make arrangements for that child to visit their future classroom.

The library is open to pre-schoolers and their parents every morning between eight-thirty and nine. On our "Wonderful Wednesdays", parents and their pre-school children can spend time in the library from nine to ten-thirty, building the children's love of books and reading. Both programmes are supervised by a teacher from the year 1 to 3 syndicate.

We invest significant time in the actual process of enrolment, which is used as a time to clarify expectations and to discuss with the parents what they want for their child. During the enrolment visit, the parents are informed about what happens at the school and what to expect (if they are not already familiar with the details). The visit is also used to gain relevant information about the child's home and family and to observe the child manipulating equipment and playing with a range of materials.

Four weeks later, we follow up with a check using the School Entry Assessment kit and other tools, again sharing data with the parents.

Further reading

Studies and commentary about effective partnerships and their impact on student motivation and achievement include:

Cairney, T. H. and Munsie, L. (1995). "Parent Participation in Literacy Learning".

Glynn, T., Berryman, M., and Glynn, V. (2000). *The Rotorua Home and School Literacy Project.*

Hargreaves, A. (2000). "Four Ages of Professionalism and Professional Learning".

McNaughton, S. (1995). *Patterns of Emergent Literacy: Processes of Development and Transition.*

McNaughton, S. (2002). *Meeting of Minds.*

Ministry of Education (1999a). *Literacy Experts Group Report to the Secretary for Education.*

Ministry of Education (2003a). *Quality Teaching for Diverse Students in Schooling: Best Evidence Synthesis.*

Ministry of Education (2003c). *The Home-School Partnership Programme: Literacy Focus.*

Nechyba, T. P., McEwan, P., and Older-Aguilar, D. (2000). *The Impact of Family and Community Resources on Student Outcomes: Report to the Ministry of Education (Strategic Research Initiative Literature Review).*

Phillips, G., McNaughton, S., and MacDonald, S. (2000). *Picking up the Pace: Effective Literacy Interventions for Accelerated Progress over the Transition into Decile 1 Schools.*

Snow, C. E., Burns, S. M., and Griffin, P., eds (1998). *Preventing Reading Difficulties in Young Children.*

Turoa, L., Wolfgramm, E., Tanielu, L., and McNaughton, S. (2002). *Pathways over the Transition to Schools: Studies in Family Literacy Practices and Effective Classroom Contexts for Māori and Pasifika Children.*

Wolfgramm, E., McNaughton, S., and Afeaki, V. (1997). "Story Reading Programme in a Tongan Language Group".

Wylie, C., Thompson, J., and Lythe, C. C. (1999). *Competent Children at Eight: Families, Early Education, and Schools.*

Wylie, C., Thompson, J., and Lythe, C. C. (2001). *Competent Children at 10: Families, Early Education, and Schools.*

For full reference details of the resources listed here, refer to pages 189–194.

Chapter 8:

Effective Programmes

Introduction

Each of the preceding chapters describes a dimension of effective literacy practice, discusses its impact on student outcomes, and explains what that dimension means for classroom teaching.

In summary, it's important for teachers to:

- have a knowledge base for what they do;
- have a detailed knowledge of their students;
- be strategic in their instruction;
- place the use and creation of texts at the centre of their students' learning;
- have high expectations for all their students' potential to achieve;
- foster partnerships.

When teachers know and can articulate why they do what they do, they can trust their own judgment and be confident in their ability to make the best decisions for their students' learning. The teacher is a professional, and teaching is a creative profession. There is a sense in which literacy is not just taught and learned but is lived every day in classrooms. A well-shaped programme enables both teacher and students to enjoy a rich and productive literacy learning environment.

Shaping the literacy programme

This chapter discusses how the dimensions of effective practice come together for teachers as they shape and operate their classroom literacy programmes. Teachers need to achieve cohesiveness and balance across their programmes in all learning areas of the curriculum. This involves making informed decisions about the right mix of components for their classroom literacy programme.

The decision-making process is complex because of the multiple pathways that students take in their literacy learning and the range of needs in any classroom. The teacher makes professional decisions both in setting up the programme and in running and monitoring it. Decisions are made on the basis of the knowledge teachers have about how students acquire literacy. Teachers need to think about:

- the components of the programme (in order to provide the right mix for their students);
- scheduling, organisation, and management, including class routines and grouping arrangements;

- their use of assessment data to set instructional objectives;
- their use of instructional strategies and teaching approaches to provide text-based activities for the range of needs in the class;
- their expectations for their students' patterns of progress;
- links in literacy teaching and learning across the curriculum.

It has been established (see chapter 1) that all the dimensions of effective practice are relevant for all students. The teacher's leadership role in putting the classroom programme together involves knowing when to take action and when to seek help in addressing the needs of:

- students from diverse cultural and linguistic backgrounds;
- highly talented, rapid-progress students (to enable them to extend and enrich their literacy learning);
- students who are experiencing difficulties or not making the progress they could;
- new learners of English;
- students with special needs;
- students who are at the school for only a short time.

Teachers also need to:

- make decisions about when interventions are needed and manage the intervention process in the classroom (see pages 164–165);
- plan for and manage transitions within the school, between schools, and between schools and other settings (see pages 165–166);
- decide how available resources can best be used (as well as publications, resources for literacy learning include people, such as teacher aides and bilingual translators, spaces, and a wide variety of materials);
- know when and how to access and use specialist expertise, such as advice from their local resource teacher: literacy or from an ESOL adviser, to inform their teaching practice.

Organisation and management

Good organisation and management of the classroom programme are essential to effective instructional practice.[62] Appropriate structures and routines help the teacher to provide the best literacy learning support for each of their students. These routines can be developed with the students so that they all understand what is expected and why, for example, when they work at independent activities and move from one to the next. Students learn best when the classroom organisation:

- is manageable and easy to run;
- makes effective use of the available space and resources;
- makes the best use of various groupings (including social and collaborative relationships);

---

[62] For a discussion of classroom management in relation to literacy learning, see *Guided Reading: Years 1–4*, pages 15–16.

- takes into account the different needs of learners, including those from diverse cultural and linguistic backgrounds;
- fosters independent learning, so that students are encouraged to take increasing responsibility for their own learning.

Professional learning communities

Making a commitment to weekly professional meetings is not easy, but it is one of the best ways to develop thoughtful practice schoolwide and to improve teaching and learning. Ongoing, on-site professional development through reflective, self-guided, weekly conversations about teaching practice is a necessity for sustained growth and transformation for both students and teachers.

Routman, 2002, page 35

The effectiveness of classroom literacy programmes is greatly increased when the teachers form a professional learning community in the school. This engages teachers in a shared process of enquiry to improve the effectiveness of their teaching practice. These teachers:

- create a vision of how they can make a difference to their students' achievement;
- build a safe and collaborative environment for working as colleagues (just as they do with their students);
- reflect on their practice;
- take responsibility for their own professional growth (for example, through professional reading, inviting contributions from experts, or working with a mentor);
- develop a shared language to enable them to discuss and describe their practice and to analyse their students' work;
- engage in quality conversations that involve precise talk about data, analytical discussion of individual learners, and consideration of what their conclusions mean for particular instructional practices;
- seek feedback from one another and give one another feedback;
- foster a climate of continuous improvement;
- develop shared understandings about effective literacy practice and what it looks like in their classrooms;
- develop shared expectations about the achievement levels and rates of progress of all their students;
- celebrate their achievements together.

Classrooms as learning communities

Effective teachers develop their classrooms as learning communities, too. The quality of the classroom "climate" is crucial to the students' emotional and social well-being. See page 11 for comment on the importance of quality interactions and classroom environments in relation to students' literacy achievement.

But the focus in the classroom is on effective teaching and learning, on goal setting and challenge. The classroom is businesslike as well as cheerful, and the students know what is expected of them. Teachers are clear about the intended outcomes of their programmes and therefore have clear instructional objectives for the literacy activities. Their objectives are informed by sound data so that they achieve a match between what the students know and what they need to learn. Effective teachers successfully align the students' expertise and the learning tasks.

Through the classroom programme, the teacher builds a learning community in which all members participate actively, learn co-operatively, and share their expertise. Such learning communities develop shared values – values that all the students, and the teacher, can identify with.

Students who are members of classrooms that are learning communities will set goals for themselves and pursue their own learning. As they become increasingly metacognitive learners, they, like their teachers, will know why they do what they do and choose, deliberately, to do it.

Using a topic for literacy across the curriculum: A case study

One morning in a small rural school, two teachers and their year 1 to 4 students began discussing eels after a student arrived with a story about a weekend eeling trip. They explored the idea of catching eels and brainstormed words for what it's like to catch an eel. Eeling is a familiar activity in the local community, and the students engaged at once with the topic and became absorbed in it. Both teachers realised that this topic would be a great learning focus to meet many objectives, not just in literacy but across the curriculum. On pages 174–176, the teachers describe some of the teaching and learning that followed. Samples of the students' work are also shown. (Refer to page 103 for more on this topic study.)

Planning for learning

We decided on curriculum objectives that were based on the learners' identified needs at different levels in English, social studies, technology, the arts, and science. The focus, however, was on language and literacy. For example, we planned for the students to meet outcomes such as "describe a process or event in sequence, using the features of a procedural text or a report" and "research, select, and summarise information and use it in their writing". We developed shared goals with the students (for example, "to write procedural text" and "to write a recount") and agreed on success criteria for each shared goal.

We described the evidence of learning that we would look for, such as: "the students demonstrate that they understand and can use the features of particular forms (report, recount, explanation, poetry)" and "the students locate and gather information from relevant sources, such as whānau, local farmers, the *School Journal*, and the Internet, and use it in their writing".

The "eels" experience

As a class, we planned a sequence of experiences. We decided to catch, observe, prepare, and eat eels. The students gathered information about eels, including ideas about eel bait. We had lots of discussion on what sorts of bait would be irresistible! We set our hīnaki on a nearby farm, and the following morning we went to check them in a state of high excitement. The hīnaki were full of the most beautiful fat, black, squirming eels.

We transported the eels to school in chillybins on a four-wheeler farm bike and put some of them in a tank in the classroom. Getting them into the tank posed a problem, and we brainstormed ways to do it without spilling water everywhere. For a few days, the students fed and observed the eels in the class tank.

A helpful farmer kept the other eels for us in a bigger tank. On a planned day, we caught and killed some of these eels and de-slimed them with rolled-up newspaper. We gutted them and hung them on a line to dry. When they were dry, we took them to a parent's smokehouse. We invited whānau to demonstrate how to smoke eels; they also supervised the lighting of the fire. The next day, we took the eels out of the smokehouse and ate them at school. They were absolutely delicious!

English language and literacy learning

In *oral language*, there was much lively discussion and debate, especially about solving the problem of how to keep eels in the classroom. Students who were usually reluctant to contribute became enthusiastic and articulate. All the students made an oral presentation, choosing from tasks such as "give directions on how to catch eels", "describe how to smoke and preserve eels", "make a presentation to the class on the life cycle of an eel", "read your poem to the class", and "retell a published story".

How I made My EeL

I rolled my dough.

I made the dorsal fins

I made the eyes

I made the feelers.

By Liam.

SLIPPERY EELS

Eels are slippery and slimy

Eels are soft and gooey

Eels live in brown muddy water

If you grab their head

They will

Bite you on the finger

Ow ow ow

Poem by Daniel and Frankie

174

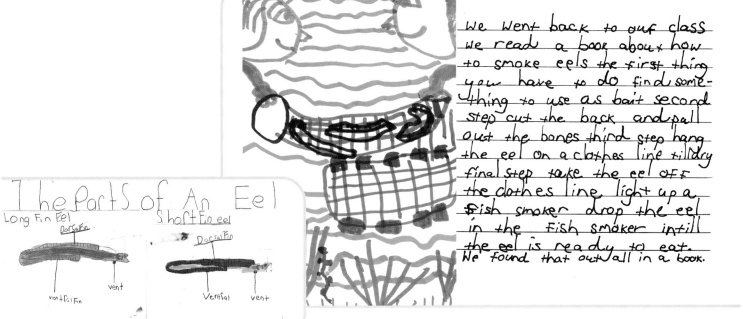

We went back to our class we read a book about how to smoke eels the first thing you have to do find something to use as bait second step cut the back and pall out the bones third step hang the eel on a clothes line till dry final step take the eel off the clothes line, light up a fish smoker drop the eel in the fish smoker intill the eel is ready to eat. We found that out all in a book.

The Parts of An Eel

Long Fin Eel
Dorsal Fin
vent
ventral Fin

Short Fin eel
Dorsal Fin
Ventral vent

In *shared reading* sessions, the texts we read included *Watercress Tuna and the Children of Champion Street* by Patricia Grace, *Hīnaki* by Jan Trafford, *Millions of Eels* by Howard Small, an article from the Internet on the life cycle of the eel, and *The Slimy Book* by Babette Cole. We talked about slimy things and shared words to describe eels – slippery, creepy, sloppy, and slithery.

For *guided reading*, we used *School Journal* articles and stories about eels and eeling to meet a range of objectives, including vocabulary development. The students learned technical terms, such as dorsal fin, vent, and migration. They practised locating information in a text and learned about the features of a report, which helped them to meet goals in science, social studies, and technology as well as English.

A number of eel-related resources were made available in the classroom for *independent reading*. For example, factual items about eels were stuck to the eel tank for the students to read as they watched the eels. With teacher support, the students made extensive use of reference texts and of the Internet. They located and downloaded eel management plans for different regions of New Zealand. They were excited to discover a site about eels posted by an Australian school, and they compared this with their own work.

Some of the *language experience* aspects of the eels topic are described on page 103. In *shared and guided writing*, we modelled a range of text forms. For example, we used the Internet article on eels to help model a report. The students went on to write reports about eels and their life cycle (years 1 to 2), and the performance of a class play (years 3 to 4). We also provided models of some forms of poetry, and many students wrote their own poems. The class collaborated on some poems and on a handmade big book.

The students' *independent writing* included poetic, personal, expressive, and transactional writing, much of which was revised and published using the computer. There were instructions on how to catch, kill, prepare, and smoke eels and explanations of how a smokehouse works. There were recounts and procedural texts, diaries, and poems. Many students used a wider vocabulary than in their previous writing, choosing words to make their writing more interesting for their audience.

Learning across the curriculum

In *social studies*, one goal involved comparing how people gather resources today with how they did so in the past. The year 3 students explored the roles people took when gathering food from the sea and rivers in the past and compared them with how people catch eels and other fish today. The students were led to think critically and reflect on their learning. They discussed traditional Māori customs associated with eeling, and this led to further writing.

In *science*, the students working within level 1 were asked to observe the physical features of an eel and to sketch and label them. Students working within level 2 were asked to investigate the changes that an eel undergoes during its life cycle by researching, writing a report, and drawing a diagram and labelling it.

In *technology*, some students designed an eel trap, asking questions and sharing ideas about the best way to do this. They used the School Journal Story Library book *Hīnaki* for reference. Other students designed a packaging system for marketing eels locally.

The older students wrote and presented, as *drama* and *dance*, an adaptation of *Watercress Tuna and the Children of Champion Street* and performed it at the school assembly. Planning for this generated much rich discussion about appropriate use of language, costume, and basic choreography.

The topic provided opportunities for use of *te reo Māori*, for example, when we shared the story *Rārāina Tuna* by Te Aorere Riddell.

In addition, the younger students created dough eels, meeting specific success criteria and evaluating their own work. Photographs were taken of the students with these.

Reflecting and evaluating

As teachers, we were able to use the eels topic to generate new learning and to help the students make connections between oral, written, and visual language, between reading and writing, and between work in many curriculum areas. The eels experience fostered our partnerships with parents and the community, and the students, too, worked collaboratively with their parents, teachers, and peers, developing social skills and solving problems together.

We noticed that the students also took more responsibility for their independent tasks, owning and monitoring their own work. We gathered evidence of literacy learning and cross-curricular learning, across all levels, that went beyond the goals we had planned to meet. We are now using this information in planning next steps for the students.

☐	I have made the shape of the eel
☐	I have drawn most of the parts of the eel
☐	I have made my dough eel with most of the parts
☐	I can talk about my own dough eel
☐	I can respond to and talk about others' work

Case studies of effective practice

On pages 177–188, three teachers tell their stories to illustrate how the dimensions of effective practice come together in a classroom programme. They are:

- a teacher of year 1 in an urban school with a highly diverse population;
- a teacher of a year 0 to 4 class in a rural school;
- a teacher of year 4 students in an urban school.

Each of these teachers describes how they plan and organise their literacy programme and why it is shaped as it is. They discuss some of the professional decisions that they make to take account of the range of their students' literacy-learning needs and also their social and cultural needs. They explain what informs these decisions.

Case Study 1: Year 1 in an urban school

A teacher of a year 1 class in an urban school with a highly diverse population

Jac teaches a year 1 class in a South Auckland contributing school that is well over 100 years old and has a strong sense of community. The school's current roll is 400, and its population is highly diverse. The school's decile rating is 3. Jac describes her current class and literacy programme.

My classroom has 18 children, with ages ranging from 5 years to 5 years 9 months. There are 8 boys and 10 girls. The ethnic mix is 39% Pākehā, 28% Pasifika, 28% Māori, and 5% Asian. There are some children who have had few experiences with written language and have limited alphabet knowledge and others who have had many language-rich experiences. Currently, the children's reading levels range from Magenta to Yellow. One child attends the school's ESOL programme, and one is currently receiving support from a speech language therapist.

In the first few weeks after each child starts school, I collect and record information about how the child is adapting to the classroom situation and about their oral language, social, literacy, and motor skills. Each child's learning needs and next teaching steps are then identified, and the children are grouped according to their needs.

At the beginning of a new entrant's schooling, my focus is on helping the child to write their first and last name correctly, write the day of the week, develop phonological awareness, learn the alphabet, and begin to record sounds. In reading, the focus is on establishing directionality, one-to-one word matching, using visual information, and acquiring high-frequency words. They develop these competencies within the context of reading real texts and gaining meaning from them. My ongoing observations of each child's progress and skills enable me to plan future teaching steps and areas that need to be revisited.

The school makes a feature of establishing links with parents before the children begin school. At enrolment interviews before the children begin their pre-school visits, we share and record information on each child. The parents give details about their child, such as likes, social skills, and what they want the school to provide. We provide a range of information on how the parents can help at home, including handwriting, alphabet, reading, and writing activities.

Children, parents, and staff from the local kindergarten and playcentre make regular visits to our school. Four weeks before they start school, each child starts visiting the classroom they will be in.

The school uses an integrated approach to curriculum planning and implementation, and my syndicate plans learning outcomes that emphasise the links between literacy and topics. This feeds into my planning for my literacy groups.

Classroom organisation

Classroom organisation and routines are very important. I ensure that everything in the learning areas (for maths, art, science, reading and writing, etc.) is accessible to the children. The children can work at tables, on the floor, or on kneelers. There is a mat area within the teaching station, which includes a whiteboard and the teacher resources needed for working with groups. After the first term, the children decide on the layout of the room for the following term. This is sometimes successful and sometimes not. For example, one year the children rapidly changed their minds about the placement of the mat area after several days of being in a draft, feeling cold, and having constant traffic past the open door!

The children's work is displayed in the corridor and on wires as well as on the classroom walls, and I change the displays regularly. The displays reflect the children's languages and cultures, e.g., Māori art patterns, tapa cloth prints, He Purapura wall stories, and Chinese lanterns. Displays also include artefacts, cicada skins, walnuts, flowers, and books in home languages. Recently, we had Mandarin characters displayed around the room. The children love reading the displays.

From the time they start school, the children are encouraged to work independently. In the first 4 weeks of the year, I focus on modelling and establishing routines and practices, from painting a response to a text and using the dough for their names to alphabet and word activities. They are responsible for getting out or organising the equipment they will need. Many of my new entrants have not attended early childhood centres, and some of them are not aware of how to manage potentially messy materials such as paint, glue, and dough! However, I spend time on this so that when I start taking groups, the children know the expectations and need little help with their independent activities. Often I identify specific children whom other children can ask for help if I am busy with a group.

I aim to have a supportive classroom climate where all children help each other. I find that it's important to provide times when children can teach each other, but this needs to be balanced by a range of independent activities that maintain previous learning.

At the start of each term, for 1 or 2 weeks, I revisit the independent activities and the routines that I expect the children to follow. I model the expectations for each independent activity, and we practise it together. Then the children do it themselves while I check and reinforce the routines.

The independent literacy activities in my class include:

- independent book boxes – the children reread familiar books and books read with the teacher in previous sessions;

- independent writing – the children practise skills they have been taught, such as drawing pictures and writing about them or publishing previously written stories;

- handwriting – the children practise the letter taught the previous week, focusing on formation, directionality, and orientation of letters;

- reading – there are texts to read all around the room, such as big books, listening post texts, and texts that the children have written;

- alphabet and word games.

Children who finish these activities can choose from a range of other activities, including painting in response to a text, using dough or chalk, or reading library books. This gives them the chance to work with others and to develop their own interests and strengths.

The reading and writing routines are visible in the classroom – there are pictures to help the children remember what to do. We talk about the need for a relatively quiet working classroom. The children know that their independent activities help them to learn reading and writing skills. They understand that you learn to read by reading and to write by writing.

We have a classroom buddy system, which helps create a friendly atmosphere. Children can read to their buddy at the end of the day and regularly work with their partner to learn new routines or skills. Younger children also have a senior school buddy, who reads to them after morning tea for 10 minutes. These older students are auditioned and trained in the technique of reading out loud and in questioning and engaging younger children. We find that the tuakana-teina concept, where an older child supports a younger, is invaluable to support children and their learning.

The children are encouraged to acknowledge their cultural backgrounds, and we enjoy sharing aspects of them, e.g., by sharing news of a Chinese New Year celebration or a Tongan haircutting ceremony. I am aware of gestures and conventions that can be misinterpreted between cultures, so I make sure to model appropriate behaviour, and we talk about these things.

Assessment

The assessment procedures I use with each child after one month at school include checks on their knowledge of the alphabet (both lower- and upper-case letters) and their handwriting (including the ability to write their name and grip the pen correctly) and the Tell Me and Concepts about Print tasks from SEA. I also check the stage of their writing (e.g., pictures, labels ...).

In addition to taking running records, every term I check how many words each child can write correctly in 10 minutes, gather a sample of their writing, and check their knowledge of the alphabet and their handwriting. I have an anecdotal book to record my ongoing observations of the students' progress and to monitor their learning. In the weekly timetable, I allocate time one day a week to work on assessment with children one to one. This enables me to regroup children according to their changing needs.

I use all this information systematically to establish the next learning steps for each child and to inform my long-term plan.

The literacy programme

My long-term goals for literacy are that my children acquire the knowledge, skills, and attitudes to become keen, confident, and competent readers and writers. My programme provides them with a range of literacy experiences based on what they can learn from and enjoy.

Reading to children, in groups of 6–8, is central to my programme. Each group is read two or three texts, which can include listening post stories or big books. But the main focus is on quality picture books. The idea of these sessions is to emulate the bedtime story session with parents. I want to increase children's familiarity with rich book language, stimulate their imaginations, and help them to make links between texts (theme, characters, or content).

During these sessions, I model the behaviours expected of readers who are enjoying stories – referring to the text and pictures, making inferences, and sharing feelings about the story. I read aloud while sitting with the group, with the book flat so that the children can see it. They often get very excited about certain features and enjoy pointing these out. I find they become more involved when in these groups than in the traditional full-class "read to", where not all children can get close to the text and there are fewer opportunities for in-depth discussion

I take shared reading every day, often including new poems. I sometimes use the shared reading approach for the first part of a book with a guided reading group, until the children establish the pattern, and then I guide them as they read the rest of the text. Shared reading is extremely useful for modelling text forms to a small group or the whole class.

Shared reading and writing together make up much of my language experience programme. We read stories, factual texts, and poems about a topic, discuss them, and go on to use the language and ideas for shared and independent writing. Often I use an activity to stimulate the children's language. We write about the experience together, and then the children use this model to write their own texts.

The children contribute to my model of writing in a number of ways. They may help me to organise the sentences, identify letter sounds, or find words from alphabet cards. They then write their own stories, and each child reads their story to me, pointing one to one (this links their writing to reading). We talk about their work and any corrections, and the child and I choose a high-frequency word for them to practise writing.

I plan for close links between guided reading and guided writing, making the links between reading and writing. My plans include the focus for the session, the questions I will ask, and the follow-up writing task (if one is appropriate). I find the *Ready to Read Teacher Support Material* very useful for planning, and I feel better prepared when I have a good knowledge of the books.

My long-term plans have specific outcomes for oral language, reading, and writing, and I'm careful to plan for links between literacy areas. E.g., when an oral language outcome for my Magenta group is "uses a full sentence to ask or answer a question", a reading outcome might be "understands what a sentence is". Or, when the reading outcomes are "demonstrates directionality, knows differences between a word and a letter, has mastered one-to-one matching", the writing outcomes could be "demonstrates directionality and leaves spaces between words".

I use the Ready to Read folder to help me plan for guided reading. During the session, I facilitate the reading through questioning and discussion, and the children read aloud to themselves.

After guided reading, the children may respond to the text in writing, e.g., after reading *I Can Read* by Margaret Malcolm and helping to construct a list of people they can read to, the children might draw a picture of themselves reading to someone and write an accompanying sentence, using the text to support them. In the same way, my feedback about the children's completed writing is based on the shared learning goals for guided writing.

Meeting many needs

I extend high achievers by posing questions and discussing issues during literacy sessions and by setting tasks that develop their questioning, research, and

information skills. I use a range of activities, with the whole class, to balance the development of basic understanding and higher level skills like analysis and evaluation, and I allocate time for all the children to work both independently and with me on these activities.

To ensure that NESB students (or those from homes with literacy practices that differ from the school's) quickly begin to succeed in literacy, I have a number of specific strategies. (I find that these practices actually benefit all the students in the class.)

- I use consistent and specific language that demonstrates and expresses clear meaning to the children.

- I ensure that my introductions to guided reading texts give the children the meaning and language structure of the text. E.g., I explain, "In this story, the girl tells you who she can read to." The children can immediately read the text "I can read to Mum."

- I begin teaching reading by choosing texts where the sentences are repetitive, and then I move on to texts where the last page changes, in order to build confidence and establish one-to-one matching.

- In the child's first 3 weeks at school, I select texts that have complete sentences (not labels) and that have the character talking. These texts generally use "I" or "we" as the pronoun. I also choose texts that echo and build on high-frequency word phrases. I link these high-frequency words to guided writing and ensure that the children practise writing them correctly.

- I encourage the children to take an active part in discussions and to respond verbally. The children contribute to wall displays, and we often read these together.

- The school has an intervention programme for NESB children, which develops their language, including grammar, and their confidence.

If a child is still struggling with their literacy after these strategies have been used, a number of intervention programmes are available. Interventions include reading recovery, one-on-one support by teacher aides in the classroom, oral language groups, peer support systems (including support by older children) and parent tutor reading. I liase closely with these partners in the child's learning.

Literacy vision

Our school-wide vision for literacy is "to raise the literacy achievement of all students through focused teaching and learning of oral language, reading, and writing". As a school, we believe that teachers are critical in establishing this process for all children in their first years at school. No matter where children are in the process of acquiring literacy, it is our job to build on what every child brings, to waste no time, and to instil a desire to learn.

Case Study 2: Year 0 to 4 in a rural school

A teacher of a year 0 to 4 class in a rural school

Leslee teaches the children in years 0 to 4 at a small, two-teacher, rural school in Northland with a fluctuating roll of 40 to 50. At this decile 6 school, children generally arrive ready to learn, with good parental support. Literacy has been a school focus, so professional development in literacy has been undertaken. Leslee talks about her class and her programme.

The 11 boys and 11 girls in my class are from 5 to 9 years old and include one Māori child, one child from a non-English-speaking background, and one child with special needs. There is a wide range of learning levels in the class, but I run this classroom just as I would a single-level classroom, and my children are grouped for learning as they would be in any class. The difference is that while the children in each of my reading groups are all reading at the same level, they may be a range of ages – I have 6-year-olds reading with 8-year-olds.

The class works co-operatively a lot of the time, which benefits all the children. However, whatever the activity, I design it so that the older children are challenged at their level, not just helping the younger ones.

My literacy programme is organised into a mix of whole-class groups, teacher-led groups, student-led co-operative groups, independent work by individual students, and pairs – younger children with a buddy.

Expectations

I have very high expectations of the children in my class, and they are fully aware of these expectations. I want to see the children able to read fluently and to use self-correction strategies widely when reading. I want to see them asking questions about a text, able to predict, clarify, identify key words, and summarise. I want them to be able to use texts for information. I want to see them sit down with their nose buried in a chapter book and enjoying it! In writing, I would like my children to be able to write in a number of text forms, to write poetically, and to use a wide vocabulary. I want to see them able to edit and publish their stories independently and to understand what truly makes a piece of writing work. My goal is to see them leave my class reading and writing at or above the level for their actual age.

Teaching and learning goals

The yearly plan is based on specific goals or "indicators" for writing, reading, and oral language at the different (year) levels. This plan is broken down into term plans, which are broken down once again into weekly plans.

In one week's plan, a goal for my children at all year levels was to use adjectives and verbs to create an effective piece of writing; this was linked into an exploring-language activity. I make the children explicitly aware of what I want them to learn, and I share the learning goals with them – they all know what effective means!

The literacy programme

I read to my students often and find it incredibly valuable for encouraging their independent reading and a love of books. I actively plan for critical thinking and look for texts that lend themselves to this. I may encourage the children to look for a problem situation in a story and to generate possible solutions, which we then discuss.

The children learn to question texts. E.g., I may ask them what else the reader needs to know that the author has not covered or what the author's point of view is. I encourage them to use these questioning strategies when writing their own stories.

Each day, reading begins with a whole-class shared book session. I find this session hugely valuable for teaching a range of reading skills. Often many of the children will work on a personal response to the shared book while I'm working with my guided reading groups.

I place great importance on shared reading. Shared reading is a time when I can explore different text forms, model reading strategies, focus on skills that I have highlighted as needs, support children in reading a slightly harder text, and (for the younger children) really develop those early book skills. I often find that my younger children will take on board concepts that I had directed towards the older children: this is a great feature of a multilevel class.

I take guided reading groups daily. This allows me to focus on the children's individual needs and to address learning needs that I have identified.

My reading groups change frequently as the children progress and as new learning needs are identified. I also swap children among groups or create new ones if I feel that will aid the children's progress. E.g., I identified a number of children who enjoyed reading non-fiction texts about animals, motorbikes, cars, and so on, so I established them as a group, with very successful results. I intend to get a reciprocal reading group for my more able readers up and running and to establish a shared reading group using more difficult texts.

Independent reading is something that the children do when they finish set work throughout the day. They always have a book to take home, either the book that they have read with the teacher that day or a book that they have chosen from their levelled book box.

I take a shared writing session daily. This may be based on a language experience activity, a piece that I write, or a "cameo" that I've selected for specific language features. This text is often linked to the topic we are studying. During a writing session based on such a text,

I read the piece a few times (depending on its length), and then we discuss what features of the writing work well and why. I often encourage the children to close their eyes while I am reading the text so that they can visualise the images that the writer is portraying. Sometimes in shared writing I use a picture as the starting point, and the children come up with words to describe the picture. I then model turning these words into poetic writing.

Modelling helps to reinforce the processes and mechanics of reading and writing. Children need to see the teacher as another learner, so I not only model the processes of reading, writing, handwriting, and so on, but I also write independently while the children are writing and share the bits I have trouble with. If I am sharing a piece of my writing, I show them not only the published copy but also the pages of drafts, with all my scribbles, insertions, correction, and crossing out. This helps the children to understand that learning is a process and that the details of how you got there are just as important as the end product. I deliberately "model" mistakes in reading and writing and have the children help me fix them up.

I use questioning all the time, modelling productive questions at every opportunity and encouraging the children to ask questions. I often start with a short, boring, one-line story. The children then have to use their questioning skills to find out more. For example, the story may be "I went to the beach". Through questioning, the children can find out that I actually went to the beach on Mars, that I travelled in a flying bus, and that I went with a gremlin, a giant, and a fairy (and so on). They love this activity, and it encourages them to use probing questions.

I link the shared writing explicitly to independent writing. The children take the skills that they have focused on during the teaching session and use them independently in their stories. I believe that what makes my class such great independent writers is my own love of writing – this love I have of the written word and the excitement that I get in reading their stories and my own rub off on them in a big way. The value we place on a piece of work can mean the difference between a good piece and an exceptional piece.

I take aspects of the writing programme with the whole class. Together, we discuss, brainstorm, and pull out features from a piece of writing – this is a valuable time for the class to generate ideas and bounce them off each other. When we move onto more focused instruction, I split my year 1 to 2 group from my year 3 to 4. While the year 3 to 4 students are editing their writing, I focus on modelling those writing strategies that are so important for my younger children.

Most of the children have the basic process of writing under their belts, but I identified a need to focus on punctuation when assessing the personal recounts that the children completed (with no assistance at all) in week 3 of the school year. I'm focusing particularly on the use of commas. The class is also working on making every piece of writing interesting by using varied and exciting language.

During writing time, I call children up to have conferences with me about what they have written. I make sure I see everyone in this way at least twice a week. I believe in discussing work with children and giving them focused feedback.

I see feedback as a powerful teaching tool. While I let children know where they have gone wrong and what they need to improve, I always pick one thing that has been done well. When they have a conference with me, I want the children to leave with an awareness of what they have done right as well as what they need to learn next. I have children coming up to me with smiles on their faces for conferencing at writing time, saying, "I know what you're going to love about my story today."

I deliberately plan ways to integrate the literacy programme for my class into the wider curriculum. E.g., our cross-curricular topic at the moment is Shadows, so we've shared some factual texts, fiction books, and poems about shadows. We discussed the author's purpose and the language features of these texts, and the children are developing their understanding of how different language is used for different purposes. The children will produce transactional writing about how shadows are made. They will also write about what they have learned and base some poetic writing on shadows. Later on, when making shadow puppets, the children will be involved in writing instructions for making a shadow puppet and in co-operatively writing a short skit to perform using their puppets.

The classroom environment

The classroom walls are filled with children's work. Each piece of work is named, and each display is labelled. I try to keep the work on the walls as up to date as possible. The children love it when I can put their work up straight away! I think the most important things about the physical classroom environment are that it is bright, engaging, and print-saturated and that the children have ownership of the displays … it's their classroom!

The room itself is divided into clear areas. There is a maths area, a reading area, an art area, and a big mat area. Everything in the classroom has a place, and the children are very good at keeping the room tidy. There are two tables for the year 1 to 2 children to sit at and desks in two groups for the year 3 to 4 children, almost like two separate classrooms.

There is also an interactive area called "Who am I?" with photographs of the children themselves and statements like: "I have green pants and plaits – who am I?" The children use this area all the time, questioning each other and identifying the people from the statements.

We have a word tree where we place fabulous words, words like colossal, vivacious, plummeted. These words come from the word of the week, which we discuss and which the children are challenged to find the meaning of on a Monday night for homework. If I had to isolate one thing that's contributed to the wide vocabulary of my class, it would be this. Not only do they use these words, but they know the meanings of them, and they LOVE words!

Our overall learning environment is a positive one. Learning is fun, our classroom is a great place to be in, and everyone is valued. The children know that they are there to learn. They take their learning very seriously but have fun doing it. One of my five-year-old boys recently jumped up during shared reading and exclaimed, "A suffix, a suffix, look, it's the -ing suffix!" He was so excited. If I can generate this kind of excitement in all the children I teach, I'll be very happy.

I've established this positive working environment through high expectations, both for learning and behaviour, through well-developed routines that the children are familiar with and that make life easier for both them and me, and through explicit teaching. I spend a lot of time in purposeful discussion and conversation with the class. I have set up guidelines and rules for discussion because it's important that every child has their opportunity to talk and feels safe to offer their opinion without being corrected or interrupted by others. Sometimes I make use of cue cards in discussions, with statements like: "Can I make a point, please …?", "I disagree because …", "I agree because …". I hope that I'll soon be able to let the children discuss topics without needing to put up their hand and to take the leading role in conversations away from me.

I believe in having a clear set of rules and a sense of humour with children where appropriate. Given the nature of a multilevel class, I find the children overall to be very supportive of each other.

Assessment

Much of my assessment information comes from analyses of running records, from the children's unassisted recounts, from samples of their writing, and from my observations. Running records give me an insight into each child's reading behaviours and allow me to set goals relevant to their needs. With my children at Orange level or below, I carry out a running record on a seen text at least once a month. With my other children, I take a running record at least once each term; I may take two, because the results from initial running records to determine reading levels can alter dramatically over 8 or 9 weeks. If a child is reading below the level for their actual age, I monitor them more closely.

The children's initial running records this year revealed that many of them needed to work on self-correction strategies, so this is a focus for us at the moment.

I glean a lot of information from observation during group reading sessions, so I like to keep my groups small. I also find that the children's *written* responses to texts – especially those of my year 3 to 4 children – give a useful insight into their understanding of a book.

I gather assessment information for the children's writing through an unassisted recount, which I carry out every term. I discuss the learning goals with the children so that they know what they need to do to progress to the next level. The children's daily goals for writing, in the back of their writing books, change often as the children meet and set new goals. The children share in the goal setting: it gives them a degree of control over their own learning and helps to instil independence.

I use a portfolio system to track each child's progress and to note what their next learning step should be. I check each child's progress against regionally developed literacy indicators. This enables me to monitor children reading or writing below the level for their chronological age, so that I can keep myself accountable for their progress.

Meeting the needs of all students

I design activities that can easily be extended for those children who are highly able. This means that they complete the same activity but at a deeper level. When looking at models for writing, I identify features of that piece of writing (such as personification or metaphor) especially for these more able children. The beauty of this is that other children often take on these concepts. The more able readers are expected to complete tasks more independently, with minimal teacher supervision.

Children experiencing difficulties also work on the same activities as the other students, and my expectations for them too are based on what I know they are capable of and on challenging them. These children receive a lot more direction and support from me, and each has a working buddy to whom they can go for help. In one of my current groups, each child has 15 minutes a day working one on one with a teacher aide, reading easy texts to build up their fluency and confidence.

Another group consists of children who need to build up their high-frequency word banks. This group works with the teacher aide once a week. Each child writes as many words as they know in 5 minutes, and their total is updated on an individual graph each week so that they can each see their personal total growing.

In the current term, two boys in the class are on reading recovery. The reading recovery teacher and I decided to use this intervention after reviewing the level that the boys had reached after a significant time at school. I have already started to notice some wonderful progress by these children.

I believe that the way to provide a sound literacy programme for children is to ensure that they realise they are valued as individuals, to challenge them and enable them to achieve success, to give them positive feedback about their work to meet their individual goals, and to let them know it's OK to take risks and make mistakes (because that is how we learn). They need to feel safe enough in the learning environment to take such risks.

Case Study 3: Year 4 in an urban school

A teacher of a year 4 class in an urban school

Cathey teaches a year 4 class in a decile 1 multicultural, multi-ethnic school in an urban community with a high level of transience. In this case study, Cathey describes her class, her literacy programme, and the learning environment that she creates in her classroom.

There are 13 girls and 15 boys in my class, of whom around 50% are Māori, 30% Pasifika, and 20% European. There is a broad range of reading levels in this class, from children currently at emergent level (or just beyond) to those achieving at several years above their chronological age.

I create a class culture that provides for independent learning, and I expect all of the children to participate and to share responsibility for their own learning.

I make it a priority to form a personal relationship with each child. Catering for the children and their learning needs includes decisions about seating arrangements, grouping, and seeking support from our special needs teachers or outside agencies. I find that there are often underlying needs to be met, e.g., providing mentorship for several children in my class who have been identified as having behaviour difficulties and who need help with anger management.

I like to have the children in a positive frame of mind before we start our day, so each morning after the register, the class sings a song. We change the song each week, and it's usually an upbeat, popular item.

As well as setting a positive tone, the songs provide literacy opportunities that are in context and for a purpose. The songs are stored in our song folder on the computer so that they can be read during silent reading. They're also put on a transparency and a large chart for reading and singing during independent literacy sessions, and they can be used during assembly to share with the rest of the syndicate or school.

The literacy programme

Each day's literacy programme starts with the class as a whole doing silent, sustained reading for 10–15 minutes. Everyone is therefore settled and calm. I have individual silent reading kits and a variety of reading material in addition to the usual fiction and picture books. I add recipes, articles from the local paper, children's comics and magazines, and books in te reo Māori. Recently I added books on famous artists like Picasso, because they relate to our painting unit in art.

After silent reading, I take a shared writing session. Currently we're working on the text features of instructions. We look at examples of instructions and the way they are worded, and then I model a text that is within the children's experience, e.g., instructions on how to wash a dog. I model developing the instructions and write this model, with the students' assistance, in our modelling book. The children then write independently, using the model as an example. During this time, I conference with them on a planned rotational system, sometimes individually and sometimes in a group. After these conferences, I move around all of the children to see if they have any particular queries.

The children all know that the particular piece of writing must contain several key components, which are written in the front of their draft book. I also give them a time frame for their writing tasks, e.g., by the end of week 2 of the unit, they must complete the instructions for their own board game. I give feedback at the side of their writing page about what they need to improve or what has worked well. They do their revision and versions for publishing on the computer. Each child has a folder on the computer where they can access their writing.

While the class continues to write independently, I take guided reading. Each group's session lasts for about 20 minutes. Each group has a learning outcome, which is based on their running records and the observations I've made about their reading behaviour. The learning outcome may relate to an aspect of processing text, such as syllabification, or we may study character development or an author's perspective. We have some lively debates!

Our current focus, in addition to the ongoing building of reading strategies and comprehension, is on texts containing instructions. The students are grouped on the basis of their learning needs as identified in the assessment information I gather. But I work flexibly. Sometimes I bring together children from different groups to meet a shared need, e.g., to find the main idea in a text.

After writing, the children move on to independent activities while I work with guided reading groups. The students work on these on a group rotational system. I want the children to have a broad range of experiences with texts in many forms and on many topics, so I offer a wide selection of independent literacy tasks that are relevant to the children. An example is "the Hurricanes corner". Some of the children are interested in the Hurricanes rugby team, so I've set up a corner in the class with a news board, and the computer monitor checks the Internet each morning for the latest Hurricanes news. There's an envelope with fax paper so that the children can fax the Hurricanes questions or wish them well for their next game.

Other independent activities include word studies, editing skills, spelling lists, cloze activities, reading the local newspaper, jokes, word puzzles, singing (using the overhead projector), using the puppets to make a puppet show, researching our current topic on the Internet, pop-up books, and fairy tales. The children enjoy these immensely and become deeply engaged in the activities. However, some of the children are still not used to having a choice or working on tasks without close teacher supervision, so we still have some teething problems with this.

I do a quick rove to check that the children are on task, to observe behaviours and attitudes, and to talk with individual children about what they are doing. Often I'll take a running record during this time or do some brief, focused teaching when I see a need. For the last 10 minutes of the day's literacy programme, the class comes together to share what they have done, which could be anything from a song to a piece of writing.

I read aloud to the class a lot. It's a powerful way of building enthusiasm and conveying many messages about texts and writing. At present, I'm reading the work of selected authors who have written lots of books, to encourage the students to read and become familiar with the styles and topics of these authors. As well as using the school library, we visit the public library regularly. Recently the librarian has been working with the students on book selection.

The children take home a book each night from their independent-reading box. In their reading log, they record the title, what sort of text it was, and a star rating, which they decide according to a key in the log. The key is clearly written out so that they know what the requirements are. This information allows me to monitor the type of text the child is reading, and it allows them to see when they may need to widen their choice of text. The star rating has a twofold effect. If they give their chosen text a four-star rating, they must do a "book sell" and explain for other students, using a series of criteria, why this book is so great. Not only is the child having to think critically about the text and verbalise their responses, but also other children will have the opportunity to read it and discuss their opinions. The children are becoming more skilled at discussing their personal responses to books in a thoughtful way.

I take a shared reading session every day, using a wide variety of texts. Depending on my purpose, we may focus on word study or on the structure of the text.

I speak a lot of te reo Māori in the classroom and adhere to the tikanga as much as possible, e.g., no sitting on desks. We have te reo Māori dictionaries, waiata, and a te reo phrase folder, and we choose a phrase to concentrate on each week. We also learn te reo Māori for 30 minutes each week, and it occasionally features in the homework that I set.

Literacy teaching does not occur in isolation. It fits and supports the classroom programme. I see literacy as being part of every aspect of the curriculum. Our current topic is Healthy Eating, and I'm linking this with our literacy focus and with our work in ICT. I've challenged the children to create instructions on how to make a sandwich. They are to do this in Word first and then PowerPoint, and we'll compile a class "healthy sandwich" recipe book as a slide show. This has taken on a life of its own and meets many of my objectives.

Assessment

I manage the range of achievement and of diversity in background experience in my class through detailed gathering of assessment information. This includes ongoing monitoring, using information from the children's previous teachers, gathering observations and anecdotal notes, and assembling portfolios of the children's work. All of this information forms the basis of my teaching plan.

I take a running record with most of the students each term, but for those who are underachieving, I take one every 3 weeks. This enables me to monitor their progress closely and to be focused in setting their next steps. After I've taken the running record, the student and I go through it. We talk about any errors they made and how they fixed them, and we also discuss what they need to focus on next.

I find feedback an extremely useful tool, and I use it continually across all activities, although I'm working on using it more effectively. I give written feedback in the students' books, and I give a lot of feedback verbally, such as specific feedback about the strategies a student uses when they are self-correcting in their reading.

Currently I am encouraging more self-evaluation, e.g., the children evaluate their writing against criteria

previously agreed upon, and I discuss their evaluation with them during conference time.

I'm also introducing peer evaluations of the children's draft writing, and I'm modelling both the process and the style of writing. They will evaluate each other's writing in regard to whether the piece of writing is successful in meeting the agreed criteria.

An intervention is currently in place to meet the needs of several children working at emergent level or just beyond. On 3 days of the week, they spend 30 minutes in a programme working with a teacher aide on shared reading and writing activities. They then receive individual, focused instruction from a specialist teacher. I meet with the specialist teacher and the teacher aide regularly to discuss each child's progress.

Classroom organisation and routines

The children know what we are doing at all times and why. We have a bookshelf of class clear-pocket files, which have everything we're doing in them. Having these files conveys many messages about literacy and how it can be used to gain access to many kinds of information. The children use these collaboratively or individually. The files include:

- our fitness file, which has copies of what we're doing in fitness at the moment;

- our assembly file, which contains what we did in assembly – we can innovate on that and prepare for the next assembly;

- our meetings file, which has all the minutes from our class meetings, so that we can see if our points have been actioned;

- our syndicate notices file, which includes all these notices, so that the children can find out what is coming up.

I have a system of monitors, who each have a job description and know the importance of their role in the class. They include a whiteboard monitor, who writes the date and a motivating class message on the board, and the notice monitor, who ensures that all the children have a notice in their mailbox.

All of this is part of the culture of the class and allows the children to own their class and make decisions about it.

The learning environment

I'd describe my physical classroom environment as simply user-friendly (where everything has a place and a purpose) as well as inviting and rich in children's work.

The overall learning environment in my classroom is very interactive. I have high expectations, and I promote independence and the use of initiative. One vital part of the learning environment is my seating arrangement. The class is in four groups. These groups are mixed ability and mixed gender, and I put very careful thought put into the social mix. Each group has a name and a leader. This grouping is useful for classroom management purposes and also for curriculum work. E.g., every group selects one member each morning to speak to the rest of the class – we call this activity Te Karere. This means that every child in the class gets a time to share anything of interest they want to, maybe something exciting or personal about themselves. I've been helping the groups to learn and practise selection processes. The children are learning not to choose someone just because they are very articulate or have more experiences to share than others. They look for someone who has not had a turn for a while, even though their news may not be the most interesting, because they are aware that every child needs to be part of the process. The child's news is recorded by a class member in our Te Karere book, which is available for the children to read and often provides a catalyst for their independent writing.

I try to establish a fair and caring classroom environment. We have developed our class guidelines, and we have a class meeting once a week where we discuss items from an agenda. The agenda is always on a clipboard at the front of the class so that the children can record any issues. At the meeting, we discuss these issues, action anything that needs following up, and establish a class goal for the week. At the end of the week, the class assesses their progress towards this goal: all the children stand on a continuum according to how successful they think we have been. Recently our goal was "to compliment each other". This was not easy for the children, and I needed to do a lot of modelling and give explicit feedback. We set up a compliments file which they can go back to and read independently.

Literacy goals

My long-term literacy goals are that the children learn the strategies to read, write, and talk well and that their learning is meaning-driven. I want the children in my class to recognise the benefits of being literate: that they can read a joke, understand it, and have a laugh; that they can read a book and relate to its deeper meanings; that they can seek information and find it; that they can read an article about our school in the local paper and feel proud to be a part of it; and that they can stand up in their class and confidently share their news. Or that they can sing a song with all the right words, along with their classmates, and get that nice feeling up their spine. I want all the children in my class to find literacy, in all its forms, exciting.

References

Note on Reference Styles

Ministry (and Department) of Education texts that are in common use by teachers have been referenced in the text of this handbook by their main titles rather than by the more formal system used for other references. For example, *The Learner as a Reader: Developing Reading Programmes* (Ministry of Education, 1996) is referenced in the text simply as *The Learner as a Reader*. Note that the Ministry of Education publication *Ready to Read Teacher Support Material: Sound Sense: Phonics and Phonological Awareness* (2003) is generally referred to in the text by its subtitle, *Sound Sense: Phonics and Phonological Awareness*.

Children's books are referenced in the text using the author's names and the titles of the books, rather than the dates, and are listed here separately, on page 194.

Allington, R. L. (1997). "Success in Early Literacy Instruction: The Schools We Have. The Schools We Need". In *Best Practices in Literacy Instruction: A Collection of Professional Articles*, ed. A. Butler. Glenview, Ill.: Celebration Press.

Allington, R. L. (2002). "What I've Learned about Effective Reading Instruction from a Decade of Studying Exemplary Elementary Classroom Teachers". *Phi Delta Kappan*, vol. 83 no. 10, pp. 740-747.

Allington, R. L. and Johnston, P. (2002). *Reading to Learn: Lessons from Exemplary Fourth-grade Classrooms*. New York: The Guilford Press.

Anderson, K. (2001). *Motivating the Reluctant Writer*. Wellington: Learning Media.

Anstey, M. (1998). "Being Explicit about Literacy Instruction". *The Australian Journal of Language and Literacy*, vol. 21 no. 3, pp. 206-221.

Askew, S., ed. (2000). *Feedback for Learning*. London and New York: RoutledgeFalmer.

Assessment Reform Group (2001). "Assessment for Learning: 10 Principles: Research-based Principles to Guide Classroom Practice". Available on the Internet at www.assessment-reform-group.org.uk/principles.html

Assessment Resource Banks (ARBs) in English, Mathematics, and Science. Available on the Internet at http://arb.nzcer.org.nz/nzcer3/nzcer.htm

Atvars, K., Berryman, M., and Glynn, E. L. (1995). *Pause, Prompt, Praise: Training and Evaluation of Tutoring Procedures for Māori Children Reading in English*. Wellington: Ministry of Education.

Au, K. H. (1993). *Literacy Instruction in Multicultural Settings*. Fort Worth: Harcourt Brace.

Au, K. H. (2002). "Multicultural Factors and the Effective Instruction of Students of Diverse Backgrounds". In *What Research Has to Say about Reading Instruction*, 3rd ed., ed. A. E. Farstrup and S. J. Samuels. Newark, Del.: International Reading Association.

Au, K. H. and Raphael, T. E. (2000). "Equity and Literacy in the Next Millennium". *Reading Research Quarterly*, vol. 35 no. 1, pp. 170-188.

Baker, L. (2002). "Metacognition in Comprehension Instruction". In *Comprehension Instruction: Research-based Best Practices*, ed. C. C. Block and M. Pressley. New York: The Guilford Press.

Bishop, R., Berryman, M., and Richardson, C. (2001). *Te Toi Huarewa: Effective Teaching and Learning Strategies, and Effective Teaching Materials for Improving the Reading and Writing in te Reo Māori of Students aged Five to Nine in Māori-medium Education*. Final report to the Ministry of Education. Wellington: Ministry of Education.

Bishop, R. and Glynn, T. (1999). *Culture Counts: Changing Power Relations in Education*. Palmerston North: Dunmore Press.

Bishop, R. and Glynn, T. (2000). "Kaupapa Māori Messages for the Mainstream". *Set: Research Information for Teachers*, no. 1, pp. 4-7.

Black, P. and Wiliam, D. (1998a). "Assessment and Classroom Learning". *Assessment in Education*, vol. 5 no. 1, pp. 7-74.

Black, P. and Wiliam, D. (1998b). *Inside the Black Box: Raising Standards through Classroom Assessment*. London: King's College.

Block, C. C. and Pressley, M., eds (2002). *Comprehension Instruction: Research-based Best Practices*. New York: The Guilford Press.

Bogner, K., Raphael, L., and Pressley, M. (2002). "How Grade 1 Teachers Motivate Literate Activity by Their Students". *Scientific Studies of Reading*, vol. 6 no. 2., pp. 135-166.

Braunger, J. and Lewis, J. (1998). *Building a Knowledge Base in Reading*. Portland, Oreg.: Northwest Regional Educational Laboratory's Curriculum and Instruction Services; Urbana, Ill.: National Council of Teachers of English; and Newark, Del: International Reading Association.

Cairney, T. H. and Munsie, L. (1995). "Parent Participation in Literacy Learning". *The Reading Teacher*, vol. 48 no. 5, pp. 392–403.

Cambourne, B. (2000). "Conditions for Literacy Learning: Observing Literacy Learning in Elementary Classrooms: Nine Years of Classroom Anthropology". *The Reading Teacher*, vol. 53 no. 6, pp. 512–517.

Carkeek, L., Davies, L., and Irwin, K. (1994). *What Happens to Māori Girls at School? An Ethnographic Study of the School-based Factors Affecting the Achievement of Māori Girls in Immersion, Bilingual, and Mainstream Primary School Programmes in the Wellington Region.* Final report to the Ministry of Education. Wellington: Ministry of Education.

Cazden, C. B. (2001). *Classroom Discourse: The Language of Teaching and Learning.* Portsmouth, NH: Heinemann.

CIERA (Center for the Improvement of Early Reading Achievement) (2002). "Improving the Reading Comprehension of America's Children: 10 Research-based Principles". Available on the Internet at www.ciera.org/library/instresrc/compprinciples/

Clarke, S., Timperley, H., and Hattie, J. (2003). *Unlocking Formative Assessment: Practical Strategies for Enhancing Students' Learning in the Primary and Intermediate Classroom.* Auckland: Hodder Moa Beckett.

Clay, M. M. (1991). *Becoming Literate: The Construction of Inner Control.* Auckland: Heinemann.

Clay, M. M. (1998). *By Different Paths to Common Outcomes.* York, Maine: Stenhouse Publishers.

Clay, M. M. (2001). *Change over Time in Children's Literacy Development.* Portsmouth, NH: Heinemann.

Clay, M. M. (2002). *An Observation Survey of Early Literacy Achievement*, 2nd ed. Auckland: Heinemann.

Clay, M. M. and Rau, C. (1998). *He Mātai Āta Titiro ki te Tūtukitanga Mātātupu Pānui, Tuhi.* Auckland: Kia Ata Mai Educational Trust.

Crooks, T. J. (1988). "The Impact of Classroom Evaluation Practices on Students". *Review of Educational Research*, vol. 58 no. 4, pp. 438–481.

Darling-Hammond, L. (1997). *The Right to Learn: A Blueprint for Creating Schools That Work.* San Francisco: Jossey-Bass.

Delpit, L. (1995). *Other People's Children: Cultural Conflict in the Classroom.* New York: The New Press.

Department of Education (1985). *Reading in Junior Classes: With Guidelines to the Revised Ready to Read Series.* Wellington: Department of Education.

Department of Education (1985). *Teaching Handwriting: Supplement to the Syllabus "Language in the Primary School: English".* Wellington: Department of Education.

Downes, T. and Fatouros, C. (1995). *Learning in an Electronic World: Computers in the Classroom.* Newtown, New South Wales: Primary English Teaching Association.

Doyle, W. (1983). "Academic Work". *Review of Educational Research*, vol. 53, pp. 159–199.

Duffy, G. G. (2002). "The Case for Direct Explanation of Strategies". In *Comprehension Instruction: Research-based Best Practices*, ed. C. C. Block and M. Pressley. New York: The Guilford Press.

Duke, N. K. and Pearson, D. (2002). "Effective Practices for Developing Reading Comprehension". In *What Research Has to Say about Reading Instruction*, ed. A. E. Farstrup and S. J. Samuels. Newark, Del.: International Reading Association.

Dymock, S. and Nicholson, T. (1999). *Reading Comprehension. What Is It? How Do You Teach It?* Wellington: New Zealand Council for Educational Research.

Dyson, A. H. (1997). *Writing Superheroes: Contemporary Childhood, Popular Culture, and Classroom Literacy.* New York: Teachers College Press.

Dyson, A. H. (1999a). "Transforming Transfer: Unruly Children, Contrary Texts and the Persistence of the Pedagogical Order". In *Review of Research in Education 24*, ed. A. Iran-Nejad and P. D. Pearson. Washington, DC: American Educational Research Association.

Dyson, A. H. (1999b). "Writing (Dallas) Cowboys: A Dialogic Perspective on the 'What Did I Write?' Question". In *Stirring the Waters: The Influence of Marie Clay*, ed. J. S. Gaffney and B. J. Askew. Portsmouth, NH: Heinemann.

Education Review Office (2002). *Māori Students: Schools Making a Difference.* Wellington: Education Review Office. Available on the Internet at www.ero.govt.nz/Publications/pubs2002/MaoriStudents.htm

Edwards-Groves, C. (1999). "Explicit Teaching: Focusing Teacher Talk on Literacy". *Pen*, no. 118, pp. 1–8.

Elley, W. (2000). STAR: *Supplementary Test of Achievement in Reading for Years 4–6.* Wellington: New Zealand Council for Educational Research.

Farstrup, A. E. and Samuels, S. J., eds (2002). *What Research Has to Say about Reading Instruction.* Newark, Del.: International Reading Association.

Flockton, L. and Crooks, T. (1999). *Writing Assessment Results 1998.* National Education Monitoring Report 12. Dunedin: Education Assessment Research Unit, University of Otago.

Flockton, L. and Crooks, T. (2001). *Reading and Speaking Assessment Results 2000.* National Education Monitoring Report 19. Dunedin: Education Assessment Research Unit, University of Otago.

Fullan, M. (2001). *Leading in a Culture of Change.* San Francisco: Jossey-Bass.

Gambrell, L. B. and Koskinen, P. S. (2002). "Imagery: A Strategy for Enhancing Comprehension". In *Comprehension Instruction: Research-based Best Practices*, ed. C. C. Block and M. Pressley. New York: The Guilford Press.

Gambrell, L. B., Morrow, L. M., Neuman, S. B., and Pressley, M., eds (1999). *Best Practices in Literacy Instruction*. New York: The Guilford Press.

Gee, J. P. (1998). "Foreword". In *The Misteaching of Academic Discourses: The Politics of Language in the Classroom*, ed. L. I. Bartolome. Boulder: Westview Press.

Glynn, T., Atvars, K., and O'Brien, K (1999). *Culturally Appropriate Strategies for Assisting Māori Students Experiencing Learning and Behavioural Difficulties*. Wellington: Ministry of Education.

Glynn, T., Berryman, M., and Glynn, V. (2000). *The Rotorua Home and School Literacy Project*. Wellington: Rotorua Energy Charitable Trust and Ministry of Education.

Guthrie, J. T. and Wigfield, A., eds (1999). "Special Issue: How Motivation Fits into a Science of Reading". *Scientific Studies of Reading*, vol. 3 no. 3, pp. 199-281.

Hargreaves, A. (2000). "Four Ages of Professionalism and Professional Learning". *Teachers and Teaching: History and Practice*, vol. 6 no. 2, pp. 151-182.

Hattie, J. (1999). "Influences on Student Learning". Inaugural professorial lecture presented at the University of Auckland, 2 August. Available on the Internet at www.arts.auckland.ac.nz/edu/staff/jhattie/Inaugural.html

Hill, J. and Hawk, K. (2000). "Four Conceptual Clues to Motivating Students: Learning from the Practice of Effective Teachers in Low Decile, Multicultural Schools." Paper presented to the New Zealand Association for Research in Education Conference, Waikato.

Hohepa, M. (1993). *Preferred Pedagogies and Language Interactions in te Kōhanga Reo*. Monograph 13. Auckland: Research Unit for Māori Education, University of Auckland.

Hood, H. (1997). *Left to Write Too*. Auckland: Berkley Curriculum Publishing.

International Association for the Evaluation of Educational Achievement (2000). *Framework and Specifications for PIRLS Assessment 2001: PIRLS Progress in International Reading Literacy Study*. Chestnut Hill, Mass.: International Study Center, Lynch School of Education, Boston College.

Johnston, P. H. (1992). *Constructive Evaluation of Literacy Activity*. White Plains, NY: Longman.

Johnston, P. H. (1997). *Knowing Literacy: Constructive Literacy Assessment*. York, Maine: Stenhouse Publishers.

Keene, E. O. and Zimmerman, S. (1997). *Mosaic of Thought: Teaching Comprehension in a Reader's Workshop*. Portsmouth, NH: Heinemann.

Keith, M. (2002). *Picking up the Pace: A Summary*. Auckland: Ministry of Education.

Ladson-Billings, G. (1994). *The Dream Keepers: Successful Teachers of African American Children*. San Francisco: Jossey-Bass.

Luke, A. and Freebody, P. (1999). "A Map of Possible Practices: Further Notes on the Four Resources Model". *Practically Primary*, vol. 4 no. 2, pp. 5-8.

McNaughton, S. (1995). *Patterns of Emergent Literacy: Processes of Development and Transition*. Auckland: Oxford University Press.

McNaughton, S. (1996). Ways of Parenting and Cultural Identity". *Culture and Psychology*, vol. 2 no 2., pp. 173-201.

McNaughton, S. (1999). "Developmental Diversity and Beginning Literacy Instruction at School". In *Stirring the Waters: The Influence of Marie Clay*, ed. J. S. Gaffney and B. J. Askew. Portsmouth, NH: Heinemann.

McNaughton, S. (2001). "Asking the Right Questions: What Learning Do We Value and What Contexts Enable That Learning?" Paper presented at the New Zealand Reading Association 25th Annual Conference, Nelson, 23-26 September 2001. Available on the Internet at www.arts.auckland.ac.nz/iri/wfrc/newsletter.htm (Also published in *Reading Forum* (2002), no. 1, pp. 7-17.)

McNaughton, S. (2002). *Meeting of Minds*. Wellington: Learning Media.

McQuillan, J. (1998). *The Literacy Crisis: False Claims, Real Solutions*. Portsmouth, NH: Heinemann.

Medwell, J., Wray, D., Poulson, L., and Fox, R. (1998). *Effective Teachers of Literacy: Final Report to the Teacher Training Agency*. Exeter: University of Exeter.

Ministry of Education (1992). *Dancing with the Pen*. Wellington: Learning Media.

Ministry of Education (1993). *Reciprocal Teaching: Extending Reading Strategies*. Wellington: Learning Media. (video)

Ministry of Education (1994). *English in the New Zealand Curriculum*. Wellington: Learning Media.

Ministry of Education (1996a). *Exploring Language: A Handbook for Teachers*. Wellington: Learning Media.

Ministry of Education (1996b). *The Learner as a Reader: Developing Reading Programmes*. Wellington: Learning Media.

Ministry of Education (1997a). *AKA: Aro matawai Urunga-ā-Kura*. Wellington: Learning Media.

Ministry of Education (1997b). *Reading and Beyond: Discovering Language through Ready to Read*. Wellington: Learning Media.

Ministry of Education (1997c). *SEA: School Entry Assessment*. Wellington: Learning Media.

Ministry of Education (1998). *School Entry Assessment: The First National Picture - July 1997-May 1998*. Compiled by A. Gilmore. Wellington: Ministry of Education.

Ministry of Education (1999a). *Literacy Experts Group Report to the Secretary for Education*. Wellington: Ministry of Education.

Ministry of Education (1999b). *Non-English-Speaking-Background Students: A Handbook for Schools*. Wellington: Learning Media.

Ministry of Education (1999c). *Report of the Literacy Taskforce*. Wellington: Ministry of Education.

Ministry of Education (2000). *Using Running Records*. Wellington: Learning Media.

Ministry of Education (2001a). "Programme for International Student Assessment". Available on the Internet at www.minedu.govt.nz/goto/pisa

Ministry of Education (2001b). *Ready to Read Teacher Support Material: Emergent Level*. Wellington: Learning Media.

Ministry of Education (2001c). *School Entry Assessment June 1997–December 2000*. Wellington: Ministry of Education.

Ministry of Education (2002a). *English for Speakers of Other Languages: Information for Schools*. Wellington: Learning Media. (folder)

Ministry of Education (2002b). *Ready to Read Teacher Support Material: Early Levels*. Wellington: Learning Media.

Ministry of Education (2002c). *Guided Reading*. Wellington: Learning Media. (See Thompson, L.M. (2002) for details of the book in this kit.)

Ministry of Education (2003a). *Quality Teaching for Diverse Students in Schooling: Best Evidence Synthesis*. Report from the Medium Term Strategy Policy Division. Wellington: Ministry of Education.

Ministry of Education (2003b). *Ready to Read Teacher Support Material: Sound Sense: Phonics and Phonological Awareness*. Wellington: Learning Media.

Ministry of Education (2003c). *The Home-School Partnership Programme: Literacy Focus*. Wellington: Learning Media.

Ministry of Education (2003d). *The New Zealand Curriculum Exemplars*. Wellington: Learning Media and the Learning Centre Trust of New Zealand. Available on the Internet at www.tki.org.nz/r/assessment/exemplars/index_e.php

Ministry of Education and the University of Auckland (2003). *Assessment Tools for Teaching and Learning: He Pūnaha Aromatawai mō te Whakaako me te Ako*. Version 2. Wellington: Learning Media. (CD-ROM)

Mitchell, L., Cameron, M., and Wylie, C. (2002). *Sustaining School Improvement: Ten Primary Schools' Journeys. A Summary*. Wellington: New Zealand Council for Educational Research.

Mooney, M. (1988). *Developing Life-long Readers*. Wellington: Department of Education.

Mooney, M. (2001). *Text Forms and Features: A Resource for Intentional Teaching*. Katonah, NY: Richard C. Owen.

Morrow, L. M. and Asbury, E. (1999). "Best Practices for a Balanced Early Literacy Program". In *Best Practices in Literacy Instruction*, ed. L. B. Gambrell, L. M. Morrow, S. B. Neuman, and M. Pressley. New York: The Guilford Press.

National Education Monitoring Project (NEMP) website at http://nemp.otago.ac.nz/

National Institute of Child Health and Human Development (2000). *Report of the National Reading Panel: Teaching Children to Read: An Evidence-Based Assessment of the Scientific Research Literature on Reading and Its Implications for Reading Instruction* (NIH Publication No. 00-4769). Washington, DC: United States Government Printing Office. Available on the Internet at www.nichd.nih.gov/publications/pubskey.cfm?from=nrp

Nechyba, T. P., McEwan, P., and Older-Aguilar, D. (2000). *The Impact of Family and Community Resources on Student Outcomes: Report to the Ministry of Education (Strategic Research Initiative Literature Review)*. Wellington: Ministry of Education.

Nicholson, T. and Tan, A. (1999). "Proficient Word Identification for Comprehension". In *Learning to Read: Beyond Phonics and Whole Language*, ed. G. B. Thompson and T. Nicholson. Newark, Del.: International Reading Association; and New York: Teachers College Press.

Nuthall, G. (1999). "Learning How to Learn: The Evolution of Students' Minds through the Social Processes and Culture of the Classroom". *International Journal of Educational Research*, vol. 31 no. 3, pp. 139–256.

Palincsar, A. S. and Brown, A. L. (1984). "Reciprocal Teaching of Comprehension-fostering and Comprehension-monitoring Activities". In *Cognition and Instruction*, vol. 1, pp. 117–175.

Parkes, B. (2002). *Read It Again! Revisiting Shared Reading*. York, Maine: Stenhouse Publishers.

Phillips, G., McNaughton, S., and MacDonald, S. (2000). *Picking up the Pace: Effective Literacy Interventions for Accelerated Progress over the Transition into Decile 1 Schools*. Wellington: Ministry of Education.

Pitches, N., Thompson, L., and Watson, S. (2002). *How Well Do New Zealand Children Read?* Education Now series. Wellington: Learning Media. Available on the Internet at www.learningmedia.com/download/educnow1.pdf

Pressley, M. (2001). "Comprehension Instruction: What Makes Sense Now, What Might Make Sense Soon". *Reading Online*, vol. 5 no. 2. Available on the Internet at www.readingonline.org/articles/art_index.asp?HREF=handbook/pressley/index.html

Pressley, M. (2002a). "Comprehension Strategies Instruction: A Turn-of-the-Century Status Report". In *Comprehension Instruction: Research-based Best Practices*, ed. C. C. Block and M. Pressley. New York: The Guilford Press.

Pressley, M. (2002b). "Metacognition and Self-regulated Comprehension". In *What Research Has to Say about Reading Instruction*, ed. A. E. Farstrup and S. J. Samuels. Newark, Del.: International Reading Association.

Pressley, M. (2002c). *Reading Instruction That Works: The Case for Balanced Teaching*. New York: The Guilford Press.

Pressley, M., Allington, R. L., Wharton-McDonald, R., Block, C. C., and Morrow, L. M. (2001). *Learning to Read: Lessons from Exemplary First-grade Classrooms.* New York: The Guilford Press.

Progressive Achievement Tests (PATs) website at www.nzcer.org.nz/tests/nzcertest.htm

Ramey, C. T. and Ramey, S. L. (1998). "Early Intervention and Early Experience". *American Psychologist*, vol. 53 no. 2, pp. 109-120.

Rivalland, J. (2000). "Finding a Balance for the Year 2000 and Beyond". Available on the Internet at www.alea.edu.au/jriver.htm

Rogoff, B. (1990). *Apprenticeship in Thinking: Cognitive Development in Social Context.* Oxford: Oxford University Press.

Routman, R. (2002). "Teacher Talk". *Educational Leadership*, vol. 59 no. 6, pp. 32-35.

Sadler, D. R. (1989). "Formative Assessment and the Design of Instructional Systems". *Instructional Science*, vol. 18, pp. 119-144.

Samuels, S. J. (2002). "Reading Fluency: Its Development and Assessment". In *What Research Has to Say about Reading Instruction*, ed. A. E. Farstrup and S. J. Samuels. Newark, Del.: International Reading Association.

School Journal Teachers' Notes (2001–). Wellington: Learning Media for the Ministry of Education.

Smith, J. and Elley, W. (1997a). *How Children Learn to Read.* Auckland: Longman.

Smith, J. and Elley, W. (1997b). *How Children Learn to Write.* Auckland: Longman.

Snow, C. (chair) and RAND Reading Study Group (2001). *Reading for Understanding: Toward an R & D Program in Reading Comprehension.* Santa Monica: RAND.

Snow, C. E., Burns, S. M., and Griffin, P., eds (1998). *Preventing Reading Difficulties in Young Children.* Washington, DC: National Academies Press. Also available on the Internet at http://books.nap.edu/books/030906418X/html/index.html

Stahl, S., Osborn, J., and Lehr, F. (1990). *Beginning to Read: Thinking and Learning about Print, A Summary.* Urbana-Champaign, Ill.: The Center for the Study of Reading at the University of Illinois.

Sutton, R. (1995). *Assessment for Learning.* Salford: RS Publications.

Sutton, R. (1997). *The Learning School.* Salford: RS Publications.

Sweet, A. P. and Snow, C. E. (2003). *Rethinking Reading Comprehension.* New York: The Guilford Press.

Te Kete Ipurangi website at www.tki.org.nz

Templeton, S. and Morris, D. (1999). "Questions Teachers Ask about Spelling". *Reading Research Quarterly*, vol. 34 no. 1, pp. 102-112.

The New London Group (1996). "A Pedagogy of Multiliteracies: Designing Social Futures". *Harvard Educational Review*, vol. 66 no. 1, pp. 60-92.

Thompson, L. M. (2002). *Guided Reading: Years 1-4.* Wellington: Learning Media for the Ministry of Education.

Thompson, L. M., Thornley, C., and McIlwrick, R. (1997). *Shared Reading Teachers' Resource Book.* Wellington: Learning Media.

Timperley, H. S. and Robinson, V. M. J. (2001). *Achieving School Improvement through Challenging and Changing Teachers' Schema.* Auckland: School of Education, University of Auckland.

Timperley, H. S., Robinson, V. M. J., and Bullard, T. (1999). *Strengthening Education in Māngere and Ōtara Evaluation: First Evaluation Report.* Wellington: Ministry of Education.

Tongati'o, L. (1994). *Challenging Success: Developing Pacific Islands Education in Aotearoa, New Zealand.* Wellington: Pule Maata Pasefika, Ministry of Education.

Trabasso, T. and Bouchard, E. (2002). "Teaching Readers How to Comprehend Text Strategically". In *Comprehension Instruction: Research-based Best Practices*, ed. C. C. Block and M. Pressley. New York: The Guilford Press.

Tuafuti, P. (1997). "Teaching Practices for Bilingual Classrooms: Which Are Most Successful?" *Many Voices*, no. 10, pp. 15-19.

Tuafuti, P. (2000). "Bridging the Dichotomy between Modern and Traditional Literacies in Sāmoan and English". *Many Voices*, no. 15, pp. 10-14.

Tunmer, W. E. and Chapman, J. W. (1997). *An Investigation of Language-related and Cognitive-motivational Factors in Beginning Reading Achievement. Final Report Phase I.* Report to the Ministry of Education. Palmerston North: Massey University, Educational Research and Development Centre.

Tunmer, W. E. and Chapman, J. W. (1999). "Teaching Strategies for Word Identification". In *Learning to Read: Beyond Phonics and Whole Language,* ed. G. B. Thompson and T. Nicholson. Newark, Del.: International Reading Association; and New York, NY: Teachers College Press.

Tunmer, W. E., Chapman, J. W., Ryan, H. A., and Prochnow, J. E. (1998). "The Importance of Providing Beginning Readers with Explicit Training in Phonological Processing Skills". *Australian Journal of Learning Disabilities*, vol. 3 no. 2, pp. 4-14.

Tunstall, P. and Gipps, C. (1996). "Teacher Feedback to Young Children in Formative Assessment: a Typology". *British Educational Research Journal*, vol. 22 no. 4, pp. 389-404.

Turoa, L., Wolfgramm, E., Tanielu, L., and McNaughton, S. (2002). *Pathways over the Transition to Schools: Studies in Family Literacy Practices and Effective Classroom Contexts for Māori and Pasifika Children.* Auckland: Ministry of Education.

Valsiner, J. (1988). "Ontogeny of Co-construction of Culture within Socially Organized Environmental Settings". In *Child Development within Culturally Structured Environments*, vol. 2, ed. J. Valsiner. New Jersey: Ablex.

Vygotsky, L. S. (1978). *Mind in Society: The Development of Higher Psychological Processes*, ed. and trans M. Cole, V. John-Steiner, S. Scribner, and E. Souberman. Cambridge, Mass: Harvard University Press.

Wagemaker, H. (1993). *Achievement in Reading Literacy: New Zealand's Performance in a National and International Context*. Wellington: Ministry of Education.

Watson, K. and Young, B. (1986). "Discourse for Learning in the Classroom". *Language Arts*, vol. 63 no. 2, pp. 126-133.

Whitehurst, G. J. and Lonigan, C. J. (2001). "Emergent Literacy: Development from Prereaders to Readers". In *Handbook of Early Literacy Research*, ed. S. B. Neuman and D. K. Dickinson. New York: The Guilford Press.

Wilkinson, I. A. G. (1998). "Dealing with Diversity: Achievement Gaps in Reading Literacy among New Zealand Students". *Reading Research Quarterly*, vol. 33 no. 2, pp. 144-167.

Wilkinson, I. A. G. and Townsend, M. (2000). "From Rata to Rimu: Grouping for Instruction in Best Practice New Zealand Classrooms". *The Reading Teacher*, vol. 53 no. 6, pp. 460-471.

Wolfgramm, E., McNaughton, S., and Afeaki, V. (1997). "Story Reading Programme in a Tongan Language Group". *Set Special 1997: Language and Literacy*, pp. 1-4.

Wray, D., Medwell, J., Fox, R., and Poulson, L. (2000). "The Teaching Practices of Effective Teachers of Literacy". *Educational Review*, vol. 52 no. 1, pp. 75-84.

Wylie, C. and Else, A. (1998). *Six Years Old and Competent: The Second Stage of the Competent Children Project – A Summary of the Main Findings*. Wellington: New Zealand Council for Educational Research.

Wylie, C., Thompson, J., and Lythe, C. C. (1999). *Competent Children at Eight: Families, Early Education, and Schools*. Wellington: New Zealand Council for Educational Research.

Wylie, C., Thompson, J., and Lythe, C. C. (2001). *Competent Children at 10: Families, Early Education, and Schools*. Wellington: New Zealand Council for Educational Research.

Children's Materials

Brasell, J. (1995). *Clickety-Clack Cicada*. Ready to Read series. Wellington: Learning Media for the Ministry of Education.

Bridge, M. (1991). *Island to Island*. Ready to Read series. Wellington: Learning Media for the Ministry of Education.

Browne, A. (2000). *My Dad*. London: Doubleday.

Cartwright, P. (1993). *The Praying Mantis*. Ready to Read series. Wellington: Learning Media for the Ministry of Education.

Cole, B. (1987). *The Slimy Book*. London: Picture Lions.

Cooper, J. (1999). "Freaky!" *School Journal*, pt 2 no. 3, pp. 8-12.

Grace, P. (1981). *The Kuia and the Spider*. Auckland: Longman Paul.

Grace, P. (1984). *Watercress Tuna and the Children of Champion Street*. Auckland: Puffin.

Hunia, F. (2003). *The Garage Sale*. Ready to Read series. Wellington: Learning Media for the Ministry of Education.

Jackson, A. (2003). "Swallowed by the Sea". *School Journal*, pt 2 no. 1, pp. 16-19.

Kiwi Kidsongs series (1990-). Wellington: Learning Media for the Ministry of Education. (audiotape and CD-ROM)

Long, D. (1991). *A Quilt for Kiri*. Ready to Read series. Wellington: Learning Media for the Ministry of Education.

Long, D. (1998). *A Gift for Aunty Ngā*. Ready to Read series. Wellington: Learning Media for the Ministry of Education.

Long, D. (1999). *Mum's Octopus*. Ready to Read series. Wellington: Learning Media for the Ministry of Education.

Mahy, M. (1969). *A Lion in the Meadow*. New York: Franklin Watts.

Malcolm, M. (1983). *I Can Read*. Ready to Read series. Wellington: Department of Education.

Meharry, D. (2001). *The Hole in the King's Sock*. Ready to Read series. Wellington: Learning Media for the Ministry of Education.

Melser, J. (1984). *Māui and the Sun*. Ready to Read series. Wellington: Department of Education.

Noonan, D. (1996). *The Best-loved Bear*. Auckland: Scholastic.

Ready to Read series (1982-). Wellington: Learning Media for the Ministry of Education.

Riddell, T. A. (1999). *Rārāina Tuna*. He Purapura series. Wellington: Learning Media for the Ministry of Education.

School Journal (1907-). Wellington: Learning Media for the Ministry of Education.

Small, H. (1991). *Millions of Eels*. New York: Scholastic.

Trafford, J. (2000). *Hīnaki*. School Journal Story Library. Wellington: Learning Media for the Ministry of Education.

Trivizas, E. (1997). *The Three Little Wolves and the Big Bad Pig*. New York: Aladdin.

Tu'akoi, F. (2001). *Let's Go*. Ready to Read series. Wellington: Learning Media for the Ministry of Education.

Westerskov, K. (1999). *Whale Tales*. Skyrider Chapter Books series. Wellington: Learning Media.

Windsor, J. (1999). *Lazy Duck*. Auckland: Heinemann Education.

Index